MW01613597

UNCLE JOHN VASSAR

OR,

THE FIGHT OF FAITH

BY HIS NEPHEW,
REV. T. E. VASSAR.

WITH AN INTRODUCTION,
BY REV. A. J. GORDON, D. D.

"A good soldier of Jesus Christ." 2 Tim. 2:3.

SEVENTH THOUSAND.

WITH A FEW ADDITIONS

FROM THE PRESS OF

THE AMERICAN TRACT SOCIETY

180 NASSAU STREET, NEW YORK.

LONDON:
R. D. DICKINSON,
FARRINGDON STREET.

Yours in Jesus
John E. Vassar

COPYRIGHT, 1879,

BY WALTER R. VASSAR.

ISBN No. 978-0-9789325-2-7

ISBN No. 0-9789325-2-8

FOREWORD

In 1978 I received a phone call from a lady by the name of Hattie Ballard. She was from Holmes, New York, near Poughkeepsie, New York. I didn't know who she was or what she wanted to talk to me about. When I returned her call, I found she wanted me to come and visit her and that she had something important to discuss with me.

That same week, I went to her home. She lived about half an hour from Danbury, Connecticut, where I pastored the Colonial Hills Baptist Church that my family and I started in the fall of 1977. We were seeing God move in a marvelous way. Since the starting of the church, we had already seen God save several hundred people through our personal soul winning efforts.

When I arrived at the home of Hattie Ballard, she greeted me with a warm smile and invited me in. Immediately she began to talk about what she heard God was doing in Danbury, and the souls that he had saved. At the time, she was well up in years. She told me how she had been praying for God to send someone with a soul winning zeal and a vision for the lost to that area.

She said, "Pastor Crichton, I have a book I want you to read. It's about a man with a soul winning zeal. He was a man that had a vision and power like very few people have ever experienced in life." She handed me the book entitled *Uncle John Vassar* or *The Fight of Faith*. Hattie then began to cry and tell how her family knew Uncle John Vassar well and how he would visit them often and have dinner with them.

I remember vividly what she said then, because God used those words to affect my life and etched them upon the walls of my soul. I can still hear her voice and the passion she expressed as she spoke through her tears. She said, "When Uncle John Vassar touched you, it was like electricity was running through your body. Talking to him was like talking to Jesus, for he was so filled with the Holy Spirit." Hattie said her family spoke often about Uncle John Vassar, and she realized how privileged they were to know him.

For almost three decades, I have been researching the life of Uncle John Vassar. I have gone to many areas where he went soul winning, preaching, and held prayer meetings. Many times I have gone to Poughkeepsie, New York where he was born, saved, baptized, and a member of The Baptist Church of Poughkeepsie, founded in 1806. Uncle John Vassar is also buried in the Poughkeepsie Rural Cemetery that runs along the Hudson River. His memorial stone bears the epitaph which has a powerful statement about his life. It says, "HIS LIFE IS HIS MONUMENT". It does not say his life was his monument. It says it is his monument. This is the present tense, which means his life, work, faith, and testimony still live on in the hearts of those who read this power-packed book that will burn in your heart.

I have never had another book make a greater impact upon my life concerning personal soul winning. Uncle John Vassar's tireless zeal, long hours, burning heart, and love for Christ will bring such conviction to the reader's heart. He will read of Uncle John's day-to-day toil for lost souls and his tireless commitment to win them without any concern or care for his own personal needs, such as eating, sleeping, or taking off any time for himself or pleasures.

He had a one-track mind and that was to win the lost at any cost. He burned brightly for the Lord his entire life and never lost any zeal, even up until his departure to Glory.

Many times I have taken pastors and Christian friends to his grave site and have prayed that the lord would do what He did in II Kings 13:20,21. There, certain men let down an unnamed dead man, and as he touched the bones of Elisha, he was revived and stood up on his feet.

What a great lesson we can learn from the experiences of those we read about and how God can use them to touch our life and give us power to stand up for Christ. Our bones touch their bones and God revives our life. We truly can be touched by those who have passed on in to Glory.

Revelation 14:13 "And I heard a voice from heaven saying unto me, Write, Blessed are the dead which die in the Lord from henceforth: Yea, saith the Spirit, that they may rest from their labours; and their works do follow them."

Hebrews 11:4 "By faith Abel offered unto God a more excellent sacrifice than Cain, by which he obtained witness that he was righteous, God testifying of his gifts: and by it <u>he being dead yet speaketh.</u>"

2 Kings 13:21 "And it came to pass, as they were burying a man, that, behold, they spied a band of men; and they cast the man into the sepulchre of Elisha: and when the man was let down, and touched the bones of Elisha, he revived, and stood up on his feet."

Uncle John Vassar is a man that was greatly used in soul winning, preaching, and prayer. He may be gone from this earth, but his works do follow him. Though he is dead, his life still speaks. Those who will read this book and touch his bones will surely be revived in their soul winning.

May the Lord use this book to set your soul afire for the winning of lost souls.

Because of our Precious Savior

Bob Crichton

CONTENTS.

INTRODUCTION.

WE are quite accustomed to think of religious heroes like other heroes, as belonging almost exclusively to a past age. We read with admiration of the lives and labors of such men of God as Rutherford, and Baxter, and Flavel, and McCheyne, and Brainerd, and Henry Martyn, and Judson, and we say mentally at least, "Ah yes, but we have no such workers for God in our age." Doubtless we have but few of them, for they are confessedly rare in any period. But it is our conviction, deepened and confirmed by several years of intimate acquaintance, that the servant of God whom this volume commemorates was not a whit behind any one of these great soul-winners whom we have named, either in ardent zeal, or singleness of consecration, or exalted piety. I should not make this statement were I not sure that there are scores of the most thoughtful Christians, both among the ministers and the laymen of our churches, who will be ready at once to endorse it.

To one who never met him it would be quite impossible to describe the impression which he instantly made on meeting him. He gave one literally a powerful electric shock the moment he touched him. There was such intensity of zeal, accompanied with such a magnetic manner, that the impression was instantaneous and quite overwhelming. It was the lightning-like penetration of a piety that was always charged to the highest pitch. Indeed, it was the first question that occurred to one, how it could be possible for a man to live in such a tense and highly-wrought condition of religious fervor. Yet there was very little apparent variation of temperature. He travelled from Maine to Florida, from the Atlantic coast to the Pacific, on foot, on horseback, by rail, and by steamer, resting not in summer or in winter, in the one intense, eager pursuit of lost souls; and wherever you found him there was the same burning zeal speaking out in his looks and in his words. He was always moving in his work at a pace much nearer to a run than to a walk. In his humility he named himself "The Shepherd's Dog," and I often thought when I saw him, of the aptness of the name in another sense than that which he intended. For he was not only wonderfully successful in bringing home lost sheep to the good Shepherd, but he followed them with the keen scent and the swift pace of the hound upon the track of his game, tiring not, resting not, till he had won the object of his pursuit.

It may be permitted, in this introduction, penned by one who was privileged to know this good man intimately and to see much of his work, to point out the most striking traits of his religious character, to indicate his methods of working, and to draw therefrom such lessons as may be useful to Christian workers.

In the first place I recall with deepest interest his singular consecration and prayerfulness. Is it possible for one to live for a single end—the glory of God in the salvation of souls, and to pursue that end with all the ardor and enthusiasm with which the merchant pursues a fortune or the politician an office? It is good to find in this skeptical age one life that can answer that question without any qualification. This man knew nothing else, thought of nothing else, asked for nothing else, but this one thing. When he came occasionally to work among my flock, he at once took the whole church and people on his heart, and began to travail for them in prayer, as though his very life depended on the issue. This intercession continued "night and day with tears "as long as he was with us. He never said indeed that he had prayed all night. But I could hear him again and again breaking forth in the darkness "with strong crying" unto God, and I knew what the burden was. It was this congregation, strangers to him till to-day. It was this flock, not one of whom had he ever seen till now. So Christlike was the love of this man, whose field was the world, that each lost soul was just as dear to him as every other. With a soul knit into unbroken fellowship with Christ, he had become "baptized into a sense of all conditions." He did not love men with the natural heart any longer. He could say with Paul, "God is my witness, how greatly I long after you all in the heart of Jesus Christ." This habitual prayerfulness was something so wonderful that I wish to emphasize it as furnishing the true, secret of his life. A lady at whose house he spent a night told me that in the morning her Roman-catholic servant-girl came down, and with an astonished expression said, "Mrs. B——, that old man was praying all night; I could not sleep it made me feel so. But I should never be afraid with such a man in the house." It was impossible that he should not pray thus. It was with him as with the devoted John Welch, 'of whom Fleming says that he used to make his nights such Gethsemane seasons that his family had often to remonstrate with him for losing his sleep; when he would reply, "Ah, but I have the souls of three thousand to answer for, and I know not how it is with many of them." And all through the day the intercession went on. If he met with rebuffs or discouragements, he would gird up the loins of his mind with a silent prayer, and then press on undaunted. If he had a moment to spare while waiting for dinner, he would snatch refreshment from his Bible, and then drop upon his knees for a few words with the great Life and Lover of his soul. And such was the unbroken tenor of his life for years.

Another most impressive and instructive trait of his character was his intense absorption in his labor, so that it was a real and abounding joy for him to do it. It is the truest test of one's devotion to his work, whether he is reluctant to lay it down when the hour comes for dining or sleeping. A most striking illustration of the Master's consuming zeal in laboring for the lost appears in his indifference to the claims of hunger and fatigue, as, wearied with his journey," he sat on Jacob's well talking with the woman of Samaria. To him bodily hunger was not to be thought of, if he could satisfy his hunger for a soul's salvation. To him, the parching thirst begotten by a tropic noonday sun was nothing, if he could give to a famishing sinner to drink of the water of life, that she might never thirst. " Master, eat," was the urgent invitation of the disciples. " I have meat to eat that ye know not of," was his reply. And to their incredulous question, " Hath any man brought him aught to eat?" he replied, "My meat is to do the will of him that sent me, and to finish his work." That is a consecration to which very few probably attain, to be so utterly absorbed in holy work that the bread of service shall be sweeter than the bread of the table, and the meat of doing the Master's will shall be better than the meat of bodily food.

The good man of whom we are speaking so loved the service of his Master that it was often quite impossible to draw him away from it when the hour for dining came. He would constantly forget the claims of bodily hunger when engaged with an inquiring soul. He had often to be forced away from his work, by those who cared more for his physical needs than he himself could be made to care. Flavel tells how, in one of his rare seasons of communion with God, he became so absorbed in heavenly contemplation that he was lost to the flight of time, to hunger and to all outward things. It was literally so with this great worker's absorption in his toil. He forgot the flight of time; he heard not the call to rest and refreshment; he heeded not the gnawings of hunger. Indeed, he seemed at times entirely insensible to every earthly thing, in his overmastering and consuming desire to get the souls saved for which he was laboring.

We do not say that such indifference to the claims of the body is to be commended to the imitation of all Christian workers. Undoubtedly we can serve Christ more efficiently, as a rule, to be punctiliously careful in attending to all the conditions of physical health and comfort. But it is inspiring to witness such an example of supreme devotion to the Master's business amid so many sad illustrations of working by measure, and timing service for Christ by the clock and the dinner-bell. There is a quaint passage on this point in Adam Bede, which we have never forgotten. "I can't abide," says the speaker, "to see men throw away their tool in that way, the minute the clock begins to strike, as if they took no pleasure in their work, and were afraid of doing a stroke too much. I hate to see a man's arm drop down as if he was shot, before the clock's fairly struck, just as if he 'd never a bit o' pride and delight in 's work. The very grindstone ull go on turning a bit after you loose it."

And is there not a serious thought here to be taken to

heart? How many servants of God stop their work, however pressing it may be, when noontime comes! How many ministers rush from their pulpits like relieved prisoners of toil the moment the first day of "vacation" arrives! And how many, on the other hand, are so in the toil of whole-hearted, self-forgetful consecration, that they are borne on past the time of dinner, past the time of sleeping, past the allotted hour of recreation, when the interests of souls are at stake? Undoubtedly a great attainment lies yet before us—that of finding it really our meat to do the Master's will, as it was his meat to do the Father's will; to feed so truly on the "hidden manna" that we can, if need be, put off, for a while, the claims of bodily hunger, to satisfy the more pressing claims of hunger and thirst after righteousness in those to whom the Lord has sent us with the "bread of life."

It was I think in the work of personal conversation with the unconverted that Mr. Vassar did his greatest work, and exhibited the most remarkable power. The intensity and boldness of his appeals, the tenderness and pathos of his entreaty, the tireless patience of his struggle for conquest was something which I never saw approached, and which I now remember with the greatest admiration. That old Puritan phrase, "Closing in with the sinner," expresses what he invariably did when he approached the unconverted. He grappled with the soul like a spiritual athlete. His whole bearing was that of one who knew himself to be wrestling, "not with flesh and blood, but with principalities and powers." He had every weapon at instant command, and used each in turn as with the sharpest insight he saw what was needed. It was now the "terror of the Lord" and now "the love of Christ," now the freeness of salvation, now the certainty of "the wrath to come," all brought to bear with such tearful tenderness that the effect was often perfectly overwhelming. And I do not exaggerate, when I say that his subjects generally had either to surrender or to flee, such was the vehemency of his approaches. What always struck me as most remarkable in his personal conversations was their absolute abruptness. In scores of interviews of the sort which I have witnessed, I never once remember his introducing his subject with any preliminary remarks. He came at once to the theme. His first question, after the ordinary salutation, was generally he vital question, "My friend, will you kindly permit me to ask, have you been born again?"

This method I think he adopted deliberately, as having been proved by years of experience the wisest. Noticing the shock and revulsion which this abrupt approach sometimes produced, I used to regret that he was not more circuitous in his advances. But I confess that with larger experience I have changed my mind and come to the conclusion that this directness is one of the most vital conditions of success in personal conversation. It does not require long experience to teach one the danger of starting a train of general conversation when dealing with the unconverted. For such a current once started the tide may easily become so strong that it will be found exceedingly difficult to divert it into the desired channel. Indeed, if the person addressed desires to avoid the subject, he will often do his best to prevent this result, by keeping up a strain of rapid and distracting talk and even leading on if possible into light and trivial discussion, to turn aside from which into the subject of personal salvation will be far more abrupt and difficult than it would have been to strike he subject at the outset.

We must remember that this personal dealing with men is often a duel of wills. And in this duel the strongest and most

athletic will will be likely to conquer, other things being equal. Hence it is a fair question with the spiritual
gladiator, how to get the advantage of his antagonist.
He should adopt the best possible strategy, and aim to
effect by his alertness and skill what he might fail to accomplish by main force. Hence John Vassar's method
was to strike a man at once with the most direct and vital question which could be brought to bear. Instead of
hinting by a lengthened introduction what he proposed
to do, he did it before his subject had time to gather
himself up or brace himself against the attack. And no
sooner was the battle opened than it was followed up
with the intensest rapidity, by appeal, and argument,
and warning, and entreaty, all ending in a most fervent
and melting plea at the throne of grace that the Spirit
would seal his words to him who had heard them.

The results were various, of course. The person addressed was always stunned and startled, sometimes
made angry; but in multitudes of cases wounded into
life. There was never the slightest tinge of severity,
mark you, in the abruptness. If there was a tremendous grappling with the soul, it was a battle in which
tears and entreaties were the prevailing weapons;
and no rebuffs or abuse could ever draw from him a
single impatient utterance. It was not his harshness
but his intense earnestness that so roused men. Indeed you can well imagine what would be the result
for a man of this sort to go through some street in
proud, cultivated, aristocratic Boston, ringing every
door-bell and confronting every household with this
great question of the new birth. And this is what he
did repeatedly when he labored with me. I generally heard from his visits, and sometimes in anything
but complimentary terms. But he left an impression which could not be shaken off, and from which
fruit, in some cases, was gathered years after. In

a very appreciative notice of him by a well-known minister he speaks of the habit of going from house to house with his inevitable question, and says, "I have known him to set a whole town in an uproar by this spiritual census-taking. But when his sub-soil ploughshare had turned a community upside down, then was the time for fruitful work." And that is true. The very offence which he so frequently gave, was often the open door into hearts hitherto hopelessly closed.

I must refer again to the method of direct and immediate approach in dealing with souls, in order to emphasize its importance. I believe it to be the first and almost the highest condition of success in the work. When a timid and self-distrustful Christian engages with a resolute, bold, self-poised unbeliever, there is, humanly speaking, an immense disparity between them. The Christian standing on the word of God, and resting in the might of the Spirit, has a vantage ground of course, which no natural qualities can give a man. But nevertheless there comes a grapple between mind and mind, between will and will, between purpose and purpose. The danger is not that the unbeliever will conquer the believer and bring him to his views. But there is danger that he will defeat him in his present purpose, that he will so swing him into the current of his stronger will, that he will so deflect him from his aim by the force of his stronger determination, as to thwart his efforts to deal with him regarding his soul. If we hold two globules of water on the finger, and then let them touch, one will drink up the other; and it is generally the larger that absorbs the smaller. If two minds come in contact, one will in like manner often completely appropriate and hold in its embrace the other. But here, while as a rule the stronger will win, it is certainly possible for the weaker to win—for the timid to sway the bold, for the humble to master the proud.

And therefore the secret of victory lies, I believe, in this one thing more than in any other: celerity, a rapid deploying of the mental forces and a brisk and determined advance before the stronger has had time to marshal his resources. This was the invariable method of our friend of whom I am speaking. This is the striking characteristic of Mr. Moody's conversations with the unconverted. It is all in the art of "stealing a march" on the sinner, to use a colloquial phrase. In Mr. Vassar's case I should use a still stronger phrase, only in a tropical sense. His habit was to stun a man at the first blow, and reason with him afterward.

Of course, in using these expressions it is not implied that the unconverted man is an enemy whom we are to dragoon into the kingdom of heaven. Only as a matter of fact he will often resist our approaches and do his best to thwart our efforts at personal dealing with him. And it becomes us as alert soldiers to strike for the citadel of the heart at once, instead of giving him time to fortify, while we are engaged in the light skirmishing and counter-marching of general conversation.

While we are on this subject of personal conversation with the unconverted, I wish to refer to another point on which Mr. Vassar exhibited peculiar genius, *viz.*, his skill in dropping a brief pungent word into the mind when there was no opportunity for an extended conversation. Jeremy Taylor, in his treatise on Holy Living, has much to say upon the value of "ejaculatory prayer"—the brief pointed petitions interjected between the ordinary and more lengthened seasons of devotion. This good man taught me, as I never learned it before, the value of ejaculatory admonition. He was always finding opportunity to interject some pungent text of Scripture, or some startling warning or suggestion into the mind of those whom he chanced to meet casually. And I learned in some instances of great good following these brief words. I recall a simple illustration of this habit. When riding into the country with him to attend a service, a traveller stopped us on a lonely road to inquire his direction, adding that being a stranger in the neighborhood he had lost his way. "How sad it would be," interposed Mr. Vassar, addressing him with great solemnity, "if you should lose your way to heaven. Strive to enter in at the strait gate. For wide is the gate and broad is the way that leadeth to destruction, and many there be which go in thereat." I could see at a glance that the words made an impression, and that the loneliness of the traveller and his anxiety to find his way were just the circumstances to enforce most powerfully this wayside message. Perhaps this may seem a small matter for the consideration of the Christian worker. But I am persuaded that in his case it was a very great matter when reckoned in the sum total of his success. We heard a bank cashier describe recently the habits of a millionaire who had just died. "One secret of his success in acquiring his fortune," he said, "was his economy in little sums. He never wasted a sheet of paper, or a postage stamp. He never threw in an odd cent in making change. Every loose fragment however small was gathered up." Well, the children of the world ought not to be wiser in their generation than the children of light. Admonished as we are to "redeem the time," "to be instant in season, out of season," we can not overestimate the importance of economizing stray opportunities. And while volumes have been written on the art of making sermons, let me enforce this lesson on making sermonettes, on thrusting in the gospel brieflet where the occasion will not allow of the lengthened discourse. It is, we venture to say, the hardest chapter in Homiletics to learn.

Preachers spend so much time in getting inured to Saul's armor with its close-fitting joints of logic, with its burnished ornaments of rhetoric and illustration, that if they do not come to disdain David's sling they have little time to practise with it. But the man of God that will be thoroughly furnished, must learn the value of the humble sling of ejaculatory warning, and the smooth stone of Scripture quotation. And if we imagine that these are only inferior weapons fitted for reaching the heart of the simple-minded and ignorant, let us remember that there is nothing mightier in all God's armory than a text of Scripture, and that one of these may like David's pebble hit the head, when we only expected it to strike no higher than the heart.

The life of which I am speaking made a profound impression in another direction, *viz.*, by the startling contrast which it presented to the ordinary life of the world, and hardly less to the ordinary quality of piety in the church. I pass in saying this from the power and use of Christian conversation to that of Christian example. A humble man who never spoke of himself, except in terms of depreciation, and to whom any suggestion of credit or praise always seemed painful, he at the same time gave the most powerful illustration which I have ever witnessed of utter and unreserved consecration to God. I am sure I do not exaggerate when I say that there was nothing in this world, from riches to bodily comfort, from reputation to personal gratification, that had the slightest attraction for him. Instead of being perplexed to acquire money as so many Christians are, he seemed greatly perplexed if any came into his hand to know what to do with it. If a ten-dollar gold piece were slipped into his pocket—as was often done by some grateful convert—he would act like a citizen of heaven wondering "whose image and superscription" this could be, and what possible value this coin could have for him "a stranger and a pilgrim in the earth." If I were to describe his peculiarities in this direction, I fear I should make him appear almost grotesque in his indifference to the things of this world. Suffice it to say he seemed to have become absolutely naturalized as a citizen of heaven, and to be living in the world for the sole object of getting men out of it, and introducing them into the kingdom of God.

You will not wonder perhaps that this utter unworldliness, and this entire indifference alike to the praise and to the blame, to the rewards and to the reproaches of men, should have made him very unacceptable to many Christians. We talk admiringly of apostolic zeal and primitive piety, but let a genuine fragment of this piety suddenly fall into the midst of us, and I am not so certain that it will be greeted with unqualified applause. Extremes can never meet without commotion. A red-hot enthusiasm for Christ plunged suddenly into an element of lukewarm piety, will inevitably produce a hissing and ebullition. Contrariety of character is sufficient to awaken antagonism even if there is no hostility of spirit. This principle holds everywhere, in doctrine, in life, in morals. The bare, silent presentation of a startling contrast is a signal for disturbance. When Edward Irving, at the height of his popularity, was invited to preach the annual sermon before the London Missionary Society, he set himself to work he tells us by profound study and prayer to reproduce from the gospel a true picture of the Apostolic Missionary. You may study that picture to-day as it stands portrayed in his printed discourse. It is magnificent, eloquent in the highest degree, and yet I do not think any one reading it now can say that it is overdrawn or false to the original. And yet you know, if you have read the story, what a tumult it created when delivered,

2*

because doubtless of the startling contrast it suggested between the ancient and the modern policy and methods of missionary labor. He was addressing a society that a little before had greeted with applause the declaration of a speaker who had said, "If I were asked what is the first qualification for a missionary, I would say prudence, and the second prudence, and the third prudence." What wonder that when the picture of the Apostolic Missionary was produced, the man of sublime and dominant faith, "the man without a purse, without a scrip, without a change of raiment; without a staff, without the care of making friends or keeping friends, without the hope or desire of worldly gain, without the apprehension of worldly loss, without the care of life, without the fear of death, of no rank, of no country, of no condition, a man of one thought, the gospel of Christ, a man of one purpose, the glory of God, a fool, and content to be reckoned a fool for Christ, a madman, and content to be reckoned a madman for Christ "what wonder that such a picture of self-abandoning and sublimely imprudent faith should have startled, and surprised, and annoyed those to whom prudence seemed the cardinal virtue in a missionary's character.

But if such a picture could offend, how with a living reproduction of the original suddenly presenting himself to the average, worldly, and easy-going Christian? I believe hundreds who knew my missionary friend, Mr. Vassar, would say that he filled out every line and shade of Irving's glowing portrait of "the Missionary after the Apostolic School." I cannot think of one particular in which he came short of it. Well, he did rouse a commotion wherever he went and the writer whom I have previously quoted, says truly, that his most vehement opposition came from the class represented by the elder brother in the parable of the Prodigal Son."

The respectable, moderate, prudential Christian, whose chief concern is that the religious proprieties be not jostled, was stunned and confounded by his impetuous zeal. The dweller-at-ease in Zion was indignant at the wanton invasion of his comfort which this "hot gospeller" brought. "Yes, we would gladly see men converted," they would say, "but this highly wrought fanaticism, this press-gang method of forcing men into the army of Christ we cannot endure." And so would come charges of insanity made to the face, the old clamor, "Thou art beside thyself." The minister who was harboring this disturber was often warned to send him away lest the church might be driven to mutiny. And thus as he illustrated marvellously one part of Scripture, "the zeal of thy house hath eaten me up," he received the literal fulfilment of the other part, "the reproaches of them that reproached thee are fallen on me."

And yet he did nothing to awaken such opposition except to show himself inordinately zealous for men's salvation. He, was just what the Bible commands, "instant in season, out of season," or, as one, has well translated the words, "unseasonably in season." What others do measuredly, he did with all the energy and intensity of an undivided heart. His reproach, therefore, was justly earned. It was not the dislike of methods, or of the man, but "the reproach of Christ," which may still be esteemed greater riches than the treasures of Egypt. The gospel has a phrase which we dare say is not entirely of primitive application— "the offence of the cross." It is not the preaching of the law with its unsparing penalties, or of the terror of the Lord with its lurid threatenings, that will be most likely to repel men, but the preaching of the cross. Free grace is a greater scandal in the eyes of the moralist and the formalist, than rigid and exacting law. And so inevitable from the nature of the case is the offence of the cross, that it seems to me that any ministry which is not to some extent stamped with the seal and credential of reproach cannot be true. And just as the power of the cross is exhibited in this life in a self-denying earnestness in saving the lost and a Christ-like surrender of all earthly things for the accomplishment of the one end, there will likely be reproach. It will come from the unconverted, and most certainly from the formalist within the church. For their lives being pitched to no such lofty key, they will not comprehend one who is so keyed. It is the opprobrium of invidious contrast. It is the annoying and startling rebuke, which absolute consecration must inevitably cast upon a worldly and self-indulgent Christianity.

But when we have witnessed such a life, what a charm it must have for every one that values the heavenly world above the earthly, and has more respect to the recompense of reward which Christ offers than to anything which the world can give. It is not poetry; it is not romance. It has been proved in a practical, real life, lived among us, that one may take joyfully rejection, dislike, and contempt, who has the testimony that he is pleasing God. What matters it to him if he is deemed eccentric, if he knows himself to be moving in the orbit which Christ by his own life and command has fixed for him. All that are out of that orbit will wonder, some with great admiration, and many with great perplexity. This will be the inevitable fact.

> "He who far off beholds another dancing,
> Even he who dances best, and all the time
> Hears not the music that he dances to,
> Thinks him a madman, apprehending not
> The law which moves his else eccentric motion;
> So he that's in himself insensible
> Of love's sweet influence, misjudges him
> Who moves according to love's melody.

And knowing not that all these sighs and tears
Ejaculations and impatiences,
Are necessary changes of a measure
Which the Divine Musician plays, may call
The lover crazy—which he would not do,
Did he within his own heart hear the tune
Played by the great Musician of the world."

I have thus sketched this life, wishing that I might by my description of it produce on others something of the impression which the reality made on my own mind. I can truly say that I never received such quickening and inspiration from any living person. And though I cannot follow his steps, I trace those steps with the intensest admiration. A life so absolutely given up to God that I believe it would have been literally impossible to have given any more: communion with God so unbroken that it may be justly said that the language of earth, its chatter, its frivolity, its idle speaking, was a foreign speech to him, while the language of heaven was his true "mother tongue."—However far we may confess ourselves removed from it, we shall all doubtless be ready to say that it is supremely blessed to live such a life: the body, the soul and spirit all given up to God, to win souls to Christ an over-mastering passion, all that earth can offer of joy or contempt but dust in the balance, compared with the far more exceeding and eternal weight of glory. Such we believe to be a true picture of this noble life. If the volume now sent forth shall be used of God to quicken the halting steps of any sluggish Christian, to kindle fresh inspiration in the bosom of any already zealous and earnest Christian, or to give new courage to any fainting Christian, it will have served the end of its publication. A. J. G.

CLARENDON STREET CHURCH, Boston, Mass., April, 1879.

22

"They that be wise shall shine as the brightness of the firmament; and they that turn many to righteousness as the stars for ever and ever."   DANIEL 12:3.

UNCLE JOHN VASSAR.

CHAPTER I.

THE RECRUIT.

"I praise Thee, while Thy providence
In childhood's home I trace,
For blessings given ere dawning sense
Could seek or scan Thy grace."

Who John E. Vassar was, and what, thousands knew, and they will not be likely quickly to forget. Whence he came, and what were the moulding influences of early days, are less familiar facts, which it may be well to trace and briefly tell. In character, as in creation, what is visible is often the effect of causes working and shaping far away.

The Vassar family was French. About the beginning of the eighteenth century some of its members, crossed the English Channel, and in the rich agricultural county of Norfolk found a home. Here at wool-growing and farming three generations lived, and mainly died. Here Thomas Vassar, the father of John E., was born, and spent nearly forty years.

But he and his brothers were Dissenters, of the Baptist faith, and like other nonconformists winced under the oppressions and exactions and disabilities imposed by the wedded Church and State. Hundreds whose love of native land was sincere and fervent were driven abroad, to gain the religious liberty which a country made cruel by its fears denied.

It was in this exodus that Thomas Vassar, then unmarried, and his younger brother James—the father of Matthew—started across the Atlantic, not so much in quest of fame or fortune as "freedom to worship God."

One October day of 1796 the good ship "Criterion," with the emigrants on board, sailed up New York Bay. The following spring they settled near Poughkeepsie on the Hudson, then a village of some four or five hundred souls. For some time the brothers carried on farming operations together, Thomas meanwhile returning to their native land for implements and seeds. Several years later he established the well-known brickyard on the Dutchess Turnpike, a mile or two out of town.

He had previously married Joanna Ellison of Flatbush, Long Island, whose father kept a somewhat noted academy there. The wife was by twenty years the husband's junior, and one of those unselfish souls whose life, spent in bearing others' burdens, is in the home or the community a benediction. Letters written by her when she was seventy-five years of age are models of penmanship and good terse English, and reveal a heart as tender as a child's.

The husband was a sunny, cheery, lively man, full of pleasant stories picked up beyond the sea, fuller still of

Scripture, which seemed to be always dropping from his lips, busy as a bee, honest to the core, ready for every neighborly act or office, and never happier than when, with children or grandchildren on his knee, he talked of the dear old home beyond the deep, or the one holier and fairer far, eternal in the heavens. To their memory he stands out still as one who needed to lay little off to fit him for companionship with the saints in light. From his nineteenth to his ninety-third year he walked with God, and then, while his hands were uplifted in blessing and on his lips lingered some of the great apostle's sweetest words, he found himself suddenly and safely landed on the shores of immortality.

Of these, parents, John Ellison Vassar, the fourth child in a family of six, was born on the 13th day of January, 1813. He was named after Dr. John Ellison, his mother's only brother, who, after studying medicine abroad, settled near Paris, practised successfully at his profession, and died there while his namesake was yet young.

The earlier years of childhood are commonly like the leaves which, left blank, are bound up next to the covers of a book. They may not be absolutely characterless, but little is stamped thereon which can afterward be read. Of the boy John Vassar, not much can be remembered now. He was wide-awake, impulsive, affectionate, quick-tempered, and rapidly despatched what was given him to do. All this those who knew him say. Had they not said it, so much might have been inferred. Nature never pieces together contradictions. Out of a calm, cool, easy-going boy your man of red-hot earnestness cannot come.

The lad had for three winters the advantages of an ordinary district school. These did not amount to much in those days. The father and mother, both of whom were better educated than the average teacher then, directed some further studies in the home. He was not a remarkable scholar, however, and it is doubtful whether he would have been even with larger opportunities. He had a bright, active mind, but patient, rigid application to books would never have suited him so well as hard, heavy work. To that he early bent his back. At twelve years old he is in the brickyard. His body is little, but it is sturdy, and his spirit is plucky; so while scarcely more than a child he is said to have filled a man's place. While thus employed, and somewhere about his twentieth year, an accident befell him, from the effects of which he was never altogether free. In hurrying across a rude log-bridge which spanned a creek near the house, one leg somehow slipped through, and was so badly broken as to leave him thereafter with a limping limb.

Laid aside for many weeks, it was the hope and prayer of his parents that the misfortune might bring seriousness and salvation to their child. But trouble does not-always work that way. It is one thing to worry over calamity; it is another to weep over sin—how far another many a soul could testify. Recovery came, but not conversion. The ripple of uneasiness settled down. The old life of profanity and prayerlessness came rushing back, and along the old channels it pushed its way. God was forgotten. Eternity faded from the thoughts like a passing dream.

So time ran on till he had begun his twenty-fifth year. Then he married, and moving into Poughkeepsie commenced housekeeping, and working in the malt-house or brewery there. The wife chosen was one Mary Lee. Like himself, she had been blest with praying parents. Like him, she had not yet learned to pray. He is now started out in life. His home is pleasant; his health is perfect; his prospects fair. What more can be asked? Nothing, if this world were all. Nothing, if there were not a soul which came from God, and can never rest till it comes to God again. So far John Vassar has kept himself an alien from the commonwealth of Israel. He stands on the side that is not the Lord's. And he tries, as many are trying still, to be happy there. But this smooth complacency or self-satisfaction is about to be broken up. Infinite Love will not suffer a soul to content itself always with the getting and keeping and minding of earthly things. The time has come for him to listen to God's call and throw himself entirely and eternally into the Saviour's ranks.

To this we pass. So far we have seen the stuff of which the recruit was made.

CHAPTER II

MUSTERED IN.

"And the angels echoed around the throne,
'Rejoice, for the Lord brings back his own.' "

SOME incidents of childhood are cut into memory as inscriptions are cut into rock. No lapse of time wears them out, or tones down the sharp deep lines. One such is associated with the conversion of Uncle John. He had come out to see his parents and tell them what a Saviour he had found. We were at grandfather's when he arrived. What he said we were too young to understand, and not one utterance can now be recalled; but the recollection of the scene that followed is perfectly distinct. All wept while his story was being told. Presently they knelt around the room, and two or three offered prayer. In the old homestead there was a holy quiet joy all day long. It was the history of the prodigal gone through again. Another runaway had come to himself and had returned to the Father's house, and under the earthly father's roof there was gladness devout and deep. Shall we doubt that it was the echo of a delight felt in heaven over the repenting sinner?

Uncle John's awakening, like everything about the man, was extraordinary. It is doubtful whether John Bunyan's or John Newton's was more powerful or profound. In the Baptist church a revival was in progress, and early morning meetings as well as evening services were being held. He was urged to attend these, but in the most decided way refused. Finally his cousin, Matthew Vassar, Jr., fairly hired him to go "just once." He went, and readily promised to do the same again without reward. Before the second service was over, conviction deep and terrible took possession of his soul. For a week he was shaken by the powers of the world to come as trees are shaken by mighty winds. Say what we will about what old divines were wont to call "law work" in regeneration, John Vassar quivered and struggled for days in its stern grasp. Sin and the woe it merits were awfully real to him—so real, that on going home from one of the meetings and finding his wife asleep, he roused her with the cry, "How can you rest when your husband is going right down to hell?"

It was not the record of a profligate career which stirred shame and fear and pain. He had a fiery, ungovernable temper, and had been given to terrible outbursts of profanity when provoked, but from other gross forms of wickedness he had been free. It was the consciousness of a state of heart radically wrong that lay at the bottom of his self-abhorrence and alarm; the persuasion that outside decency was not the holiness of God. The Holy Spirit was dealing with him, and hence he quailed. And when peace and pardon broke in, they did not come as the dawn of day. It was rather as if noonday sunshine were to flash out in the murky night. He obtained an assurance of sonship so bright and clear that nothing afterward darkened it for an hour.

3*

In part, perhaps, such an experience would be natural to a temperament keyed so high. There could be no halfway emotion about the man, any more than there could be halfway work. Halfness went against the grain. But it was something more than mere natural intensity which glowed in his face and throbbed in the testimony of his tongue. There was a life hidden with Christ whose pulsations, at the first, as ever afterward, were strong as ocean's undertow. Let this account for those positive ideas he held and urged concerning the doctrine of a new birth. Conversion was to him something definite and discernible. It was not a maybe and maybe-not change. There was in his sight a line where living for self and Satan ceased, and living for God and godliness began; and that line he looked upon as sharply drawn. He could not have regarded it otherwise. Divine grace had stopped him as that light from heaven stopped Saul of Tarsus, and as suddenly and as squarely he had turned around. Christ's image had been stamped upon his soul as the eagle is stamped on the bit of gold under the die of the mint; and whose he was, or what, he could not allow himself to question. That had been once and for ever settled. He was twenty-eight years old when he thus found the Lord; rather let us say, when the Lord thus found him. It is the Saviour who is the chief seeker, and not the sinner.

Like every consistent convert he turned to the people of God and asked among them a brother's place. On the 3d of April, 1842, he was welcomed into the fellowship of the Poughkeepsie Baptist church. Rev. Rufus

Babcock, D. D., who thus became his pastor, and was for many years his counseller and guide, could have told us much about the beginnings of this Christian life, had he been a little longer spared; but the venerated pastor reached the goal slightly ahead of his younger brother.

Rev. Edgar A. Van Kleek of Patten, Maine, for many years a most cherished friend, and at the time of Uncle John's conversion himself a new recruit in the army of the Lord, gives us this glimpse of the man when as a rebel against God he was brought to lay down his arms: "I well remember the night when he was in such distress of mind, though I was only a child in the Christian life then. The meeting was in the little prayer-room of the La Fayette street house, and as many were interested it was filled. I sat next to him in the first seat as you entered from the door. I never saw a soul in such agony as he. The service closed and most of the congregation had retired. As A few were lingering, he begged them not to go but to stop longer and pray for him. He said he could not go out of the room till forgiveness had been spoken and peace had come. A half dozen of us remained and prayed that mercy might be extended and his burden lifted off. Then he broke out into petitions for himself, and such begging for salvation I never heard from the lips of any other penitent. Dr. Babcock stopped with us and tried to point out Christ. He was more calm before we separated, but not by any means at rest. The next night, however, he was rejoicing in a Saviour's pardoning love. There was rapture on his face, there was glory in his soul. There was glory in that old prayer-room, too, as he told us that evening of God's own peace and the preciousness of Jesus.

"After this a number of us were returning from a neighborhood meeting one night where the interest had been very deep, and we were all so full of joy that some began to sing along the street as we went toward home. This rather unusual manifestation of enthusiasm called out the remark that people would think us crazy if we did not keep more still; whereupon Brother Vassar—the child in grace father of the man—at once replied, Let them think so; they said the blessed Jesus had a devil.' "

So we behold Uncle John enlisted for the good fight of faith. How splendidly he fought it we shall see further along. How to fight it he is now to learn. Years are to be spent in the drill-room now.

But he has been mustered in.

CHAPTER III.

THE DRILL.

"Each of God's soldiers bears
A sword divine;
Stretch out thy trembling hands
Today for thine."

Arms and armor are all-important in secular and sacred warfare, but how to wield the one and wear the other must be learned. The God of battles seldom makes a raw soldier into a great leader all at once. Moses tarries in Horeb, and Elijah in the desert, and Paul in Arabia, to get a preparation for their work; and with forty days in the wilderness even our Lord's ministry begins. The man we are following here was girded and disciplined in various ways. For these experiences eight years will be none too long.

Naturally enough his voice was quickly heard in the social meetings of the church. But he was a novice in religious things, and needed instruction especially in the word of God. Probably he was more ignorant of even the letter of Scripture than many a half-grown boy to-day. He had not been a member of the Sunday-school, nor a regular church attendant by any means, and little of Bible truth lay in his mind excepting such scraps and fragments as home-training might have fastened there. This deficiency he sought, far and fast as possible, to supply. In the brewery where he was employed, he would write down on the walls in the morning two or three short texts to be committed and thought over while at his tasks. On a shelf near by, or else in his pocket, was kept a small Bible, and when there was an unoccupied moment that would be in his hands. Evenings, when no religious service claimed his time, over that same book he would bend for hours, sometimes on his knees. Thus little by little he acquired that familiarity with the written word which he afterward displayed. Many a reader of this page will recall instances where he foiled opposers and silenced cavillers, as his Master did the tempter on the mountain, by quotations apt and irresistible.

No talent lent him was allowed to rust from disuse. Fast as he received he gave. He believed it as wrong to hoard grace as gold. Communion with Christ was only a holy portal through which to pass to the help of man. He began to talk with individuals about their hope; not so pointedly or skilfully as in later years, for tact and fidelity such as characterized him must partly be acquired. But from the start no one spent half an hour in his presence without being made to feel that with John Vassar religion was a real thing. In the prayer circle and in revival services he became a power. In the schoolhouses out of town, where meetings were often held, his help was sought. One such visit of his comes up as we write. It probably occurred a year or two after his conversion. It was a cold winter night, and the little old schoolhouse on the hill was packed. The Spirit of God was working in the district, and many were inquiring or rejoicing in a good hope. Others were ill at ease. Uncle John was at home in such a place; especially at home on that particular spot and amid the group gathered there. On these very benches he sat in boyhood, and some of these fathers and mothers were then by his side. The exercises of the hour have faded from our mind, but one association of the night remains. When the people had started homeward along the roads or across the fields, out came ringing one of the melodies of those days. Uncle John was leading in the hymn, and half a dozen others were joining in, and though they were probably half a mile away, every word reported itself on the keen frosty air. Some who stopped to listen thought the strains almost sweet enough to be the echoes of celestial songs. Let the worldling sneer or the skeptic smile at the mention of such scenes and seasons, but we will remember the years of the right hand of the Most High.

But there were to enter into the drill of the soldier experiences of a sterner kind. If there is a land of Beulah for the Christian to pass through, there is a valley of Baca too. Uncle John is to see a happy home break up, its lights one by one go out, its members pass away, till he is left utterly alone. He is to say like many another,

"And lonely rooms and suffering beds,
These for my training-place were given."

Two boys, with the wife, made up his household. The younger sickened first. He died in September, 1847. The elder, a lad of nine years, an uncommonly bright and interesting child, was taken the following autumn, after an illness of but a few hours. He breathed his last in parental arms, whispering the dear Lord's words, "Suffer the little children to come unto me."

Under these repeated strokes the wife and mother, never strong, gave way. A year of weary wasting and patient suffering followed, and then, in November of 1849, she found the rest remaining to the people of God. That cheerless autumn night was the only time when we ever saw Uncle John even momentarily cast down. Then for half an hour he did lie down and weep like a heart-broken child. Nor was it strange. Long watching had nearly worn him out. Only four weeks previously he had closed his venerable father's eyes for the last long sleep. The loves of earth had been breaking fast. But faith quickly rose again and rejoiced in God. The eagle flies highest not in serene but stormy skies, and the believer beats heavenward when the hours are dark and the tempest wild. The heart of the lonely man recovered soon the old peace and trust, and exulted in the Rock of his salvation. Like the needle of the mariner, deflected for an instant when a storm first strikes the ship, but swinging right and holding steady soon, the smitten soul turned to its Stay and Rest. For those who had gone it was worship. For the one left it was work yet for a little while. With soul new-braced let him go to it—new-braced by sorrow as well as joy; disciplined by loss no less than gain. He was to be a son of consolation to many a mourner in coming days. He was to minister to smitten spirits with a woman's tenderness. He was to look into eyes dim with tears, and say, "I have been in this very pass, and know its bitterness and blessedness."

It is of these days that his then pastor and life-long friend, Rev. J. Hyatt Smith, writes: "Brother Vassar was a member of my first charge, and for many Sabbaths at the commencement of my ministry used to help me greatly by looking me right in the eye. One day, as soon as I began my sermon, he put his head down, and did not raise it till the sermon was finished. What it meant I could not tell. This was repeated the next Sabbath, and the next. I asked then an explanation. He replied, Beloved, I have a better plan than looking you in the eye. I start even with you, praying while you preach; and to every appealing truth I say, "Lord, send that home. Lord, send that home."' He is the only man who ever helped me by putting down his head while I preached. I drove the nail with the gospel hammer, and he clinched it with believing prayer.

"I shall ever remember how gently he would criticise my sermons, and even his rebukes were so pregnant with the love of Jesus that I was instructed and improved without a hurt.

"In going out on my first round of parish calls, I was told that I would find Brother Vassar at the brewery. I entered the building, and approaching him unobserved, saw a man standing near a great caldron of boiling hops with a book in his hand. Looking over his shoulder, I noticed that it was Fox's Book of Martyrs' that was being read.

"In going out of the place one of the workmen asked, Did you find him?' I said, 'Yes.' 'Well,' said he, there is one spot in this brewery that is better than any

4

Church in Poughkeepsie, and that is where that man prays.'

"Mrs. Vassar was at the point of death. Her disease was consumption, and she feared strangulation. She therefore asked me one day to pray that she might die easily. In the sympathy of the moment I promised, but on meeting Brother Vassar in the next room, I said to him that I had made a hard promise. 'Why?' was his reply. Because I have no faith,' was my answer; 'and I have no faith simply because there is no promise.' 'Why,' said he, speaking as a man to a child (and I was only a child in experience), 'if you were the son of a wealthy father who loved you, and would never deny you anything that was for your real good, and you needed a hundred dollars, wouldn't you say, I shall have a hundred dollars, your faith springing from your father's wealth and your father's love?' God's promise was deduced from the knowledge of God's relation to the saint. In that day such a statement was a revelation to me. We went to prayer. Our prayer was answered. Mrs. Vassar died

"'As dies a wave along the shore.'"

Of this same period Mrs. R. A. Thurston, of Poughkeepsie, says:

"My acquaintance with John E. Vassar began in the spring of 1849. The first thing about the man that surprised me was, that, with his daily work and the severe sickness then existing in his home, he was able to do so much for Christ and for his fellow-men. He was a peacemaker, a comforter, a helper wherever there was need.

Were any cast down? he came with words of
hope. Were any indifferent? so earnest and loving
and arousing were his words, that the slumbering started into new life. Were any sick, or anxious about salvation? he quickly found it out, and
was at their sides. In the social meetings, he was
wonderful. In remark or prayer, his face seemed to
glow as if heaven had come down, his soul and ours
to greet. When we heard his clear voice leading in
some sweet song of Zion, we thought that never
before were so many rich gifts and graces bestowed
on a single man.

"I was in the habit of frequently visiting his sick
wife, and often carried some little delicacy along.
The morning following her death, unaware that
the end had come, I went down to the house with a
pitcher containing something for her in my hand.
At the door I met Brother Vassar, and asked him
to take in what I had brought, that I might hasten
back. Clasping his hands together, he said, 'Bless
the Lord! my wife is in heaven. She needs nothing
more.' I could not understand then how he 'could
rejoice while his dead companion lay in the still
and darkened house, but I understand it now. He
would not be so selfish as to let his loss outweigh
her gain. He would rather rejoice and give God
thanks that for her, sorrow and suffering were
over, and the eternal glory reached."

S. M. Shaw, Esq., editor of the "Freeman's Journal," Cooperstown, N. Y., speaking of this period in
Uncle John's life, says:

"I knew the late beloved John E. Vassar for several

years previous to January 1, 1849. He was a teacher in the Sabbath-school which I then superintended, and one of the most prompt, faithful, and successful.

"If there was a truly 'holy' man in that school or church, he was the one entitled to the appellation. He showed his love to God, not alone by a consistent walk, but by his true-hearted and unselfish love and service of his fellow-men. He was a cheerful, happy Christian, whose ever-welcome presence was sunshine. A cloud was never seen upon his face except when considering another's trials or sufferings, and then he was ever ready with a word of comfort and cheer. In this world's goods he was poor, but his heart was rich in love and tenderness. Of his means he was a cheerful giver. To his pastor he was a devoted friend, and he was as modest and unassuming as he was good."

Another adds:

"Never did he seem in the least degree to lack the spirit of devotion, or to be unready for any Christian service. When all around him were cold he was at white heat, when others were dead, he was full of life. He never came to a meeting however flat and dull that after a little drooping of his head in prayer he did not lift and thrill. It was marvellous beyond expression how quickly he could turn an ebbing tide to flood.

"He had wonderful gifts, few ministers have so much natural ability. At times he was truly eloquent. His experience was rich, his memory marvellous, his use of language extraordinary, his power to rouse the people seldom equalled; and yet with all his gifts and excellencies he was as humble as a little child. He always felt that he was the least of all saints, not meet indeed to be called a saint. He never assumed anything, distrusted himself and was ever ready to give the best place to another. He kept nothing back from his loving Lord. Whether he sang, prayed, or exhorted, it was all done in the same spirit; or whether he ate or drank or whatever he did, it all was done to the glory of God. He would come into the meeting, slip along quietly from pew to pew, find out every tender-hearted one who was seeking the Saviour, and as soon as there was a lull in the meeting, he would be heard in prayer for the dear soul who was kneeling at his side. Sometimes there would be three or four on their knees before God, all crying for mercy while he was pleading so earnestly in his simple child-like faith that God would save them. Rest was a stranger to him while souls were around him unsaved."

Thus, by fidelity in things at home, he qualified himself for other trusts. He did not belong to that clique of religious perambulaters who are more useful anywhere else than in their own homes. He took hold with his brethren of the nearest work he found to do, and so fitted himself for and grew into larger tasks and broader spheres.

Eight or nine years so spent are sufficient, and he goes out now to extensive and efficient service. He has become used to the uniform, and he likes it well. He has learned how to handle the sword of the Spirit, and ward off the assaults of Satan on his shield of faith. He has skirmished with the foe, and found out his strength.

4*

His armor has been burnished by affliction till it shines. Above all, loyalty to his Captain has become the passion of his soul. Now he is looking for a place somewhere in the lines. All he asks is a private's position, and less than a private's pay. He will not be kept looking long.

CHAPTER IV.

ASSIGNED TO SERVICE:

" Prepared the trumpet's call to greet,
Soldier of Jesus, stand;
Pilgrim of Christ, with ready feet
Await thy Lord's command."

HOME relationships and responsibilities are sometimes influential in keeping men in places and at oc-
cupations for which they feel a growing disrelish or
dislike. It was so with Uncle John. He had been for
many years employed in the malthouse and brewery
of "M. Vassar and Company," when the light of God
dawned on his soul. Soon afterward he began to feel
uncomfortable about his position—began to question whether the work he was doing was consistent
with the hope he cherished, and the profession he
had made. The Washingtonian Reformation, which a
little later swept over many portions of our land, deepened the impression that as a child of God he ought
to be otherwise engaged. Duty, however, did not at
once grow clear. With the members of the firm, who
were his cousins, his relations had been intimate and
kind. The temperance sentiment, though it was growing rapidly, was not then as high, either in the church
or out, as it is to-day. Then while the subject was being pondered, the repeated household afflictions

already noted fell, and they diverted attention from this subject for a time. Soon as he found himself alone in the world, however, the old queries returned. What had been only impressions heretofore deepened into convictions soon, and conviction made obligation plain. He left the place he so long had filled, whose emoluments, present and prospective, were far greater than he could hope elsewhere to gain, and in the spring of 1850 found himself, for the first time in more than a dozen years, unemployed.

How God could be glorified and his generation served was now the question of the hour. The answer quickly came. The American Tract Society of New York was pushing vigorously the system of colportage in the West. The labors of plain, humble, but godly and earnest men, several hundred of whom were on the field, were being greatly blest—how greatly the revealings of the eternal day alone will tell.

The committee of the Society recognized in Uncle John one suited to their kind of work. They commissioned him on the 15th day of May, 1850. He was not promised anything like ease. " Roughing it" was the order of that day, and the demand. He was not promised very heavy pay in the currency of earth —a hundred and sixty dollars a year and travelling expenses; but he went joyfully to a work that to the last was his delight. For if ever mortal truthfully could say what Christ did, "My meat is to do the will of Him that sent me," he was that man.

One writing of this time says:

"This was a season of severe trial and hardship to him in some respects. He was an exile from his home, a stranger in a rude country; he often passed his nights in his wagon or on the ground under it.

"God went with him over those grassy solitudes, and blessed his labors, and filled him with joy and praise. At times his joy was so great that, as he said, as the thought of his high calling took possession of him, he could hardly retain his seat in his wagon.' As he urged his way over the wide prairies, he felt that he was the most unworthy and the most favored man on the face of the earth. His heart was filled with Jesus.

"No portion of his life was more fruitful. It was then and there that he acquired that well-nigh infallible skill in approaching men, that was a perpetual marvel to all who observed it. He learned how to tell by a man's look, or by his first words, just what was his state of mind toward religion, and how to address him.

"Every man he met, he sought opportunity to inquire of as to his spiritual state, and if he was not a Christian he warned him, in the name of Christ, and often with tears, of the deceit and danger of sin, and entreated him to forsake it and turn to God, assuring him of the blessedness of so doing, as he, out of his own experience could testify. He went after men, and kept after them with a long perseverance, holding them in his heart and making mention of them unceasingly before God in his prayers, and appearing to them at intervals, till at last he won them to repentance."

Up to this date we have had little but scattered

recollections to put together. Henceforth we have items in his own letters and reports on which to draw, and so can let the laborer himself tell something about his toil.

His field of operations for a year or more was the northern, or north-eastern, portions of Illinois; more particularly the counties of Kane, Kendall, De Kalb, and Boone. Stopping in Chicago long enough to meet some old friends, and get a supply of the Society's publications for distribution, he struck out for the new settlements a hundred miles beyond. He was now thirty-seven years old, had an almost iron constitution, spirits buoyant as a child's, an all-conquering faith, and a large amount of good sturdy common sense. Add to all this a zeal that never flagged, and it will be seen that he went forth well equipped.

The summer was one of burning drought. The prairies, which on his arrival looked so fresh and green, by July lay scorched and blasted, and men's hearts were failing them for fear. As a consequence, the books he carried sold slowly, and the sultry days and short nights of harvest-time were not favorable for getting hold of the people, either in their homes or through such evening meetings as were tried. He says, however: "I expected difficulties, and am not disappointed in the least. The Lord is a present help. I pass along the highways contented with any fare, and stop where the night overtakes me, witnessing all the time to small and great that Christ has power to save."

With the autumn and early winter tokens of good appear. The more driving labor of the farm is done, and in spite of frets and fears crops are fair. He writes, "I had a most precious season yesterday. I find the people prepared by God to hear even me, and have been astonished to witness the effect produced by a mere exhortation. Truly our Lord does work by simple means." As spring comes on the snow-covered prairies that he has been tramping over glow religiously, as they do literally with returning summer. Nor is it the country neighborhoods alone that feel the tinglings of a new spiritual life. Belvidere, St. Charles, Elgin, and other towns in his district feel the kindlings of a sacred fire. Along the Wisconsin border are extensive ingatherings of souls. "I have no rest," says the toiler, "night nor day."

And yet he does not forget home and friends amid these joys and cares, for in the letter quoted from above he says: "Oh, Sister H., I never felt so much for our own church before. Do all you can to stir up the brethren. Warn them not to sleep while the world is going so swiftly to ruin. Do all you can for our dear W. and H. We shall meet them in eternity so soon."

While on this field he makes a brief visit to a family previously known in the Eastern States. The home was a Christian one, and the first evening passed rapidly and pleasantly in calling up old times and places. The host spoke hopefully of his prospects and talked over his plans, but made little reference to the subject uppermost in the mind of Uncle John.

Presently a good opportunity was given to introduce the matter, and he turned to it by asking these old acquaintances what kind of neighbors they had found. "Really," said the lady, "I scarcely know. I am intimate with almost none of them; and if the truth must be told, I have not sought to be."

"How long did you say you had been living here?"

"Five years next spring," was the reply.

"Five years next spring! Oh, my dear brother and sister, both of you professors of religion and yet living here so long without even informing yourselves about the condition of those nearest to your doors! What a pity! what a pity! What will the Lord say to you?"

The man and his wife looked at him, looked at one another, and then looked down. Then as he went on to speak of Christian obligation both asked, " 'What ought we to have done? What could we have done?' " As past opportunities were clearly pointed out, the more pertinent query came to their lips, "Well, how can we best take up our neglected duties now?" Definitely he mapped out a plan of labor, and before leaving besought them to put it in operation without delay.

Weeks afterward he was at their door again. Before he entered, the woman of the house greeted him with the exclamation, "I am so glad you have come! You are just in the right time."

He entered and found several of the neighbors who had come together to talk over measures eyeing the religious welfare of the community. These old friends of his had not been so plainly and lovingly dealt with in vain. They had shown how sincerely they deplored past unfaithfulness by vigorously taking hold of responsibilities which selfishly or indolently had been shirked. They had scoured the region round about. They had ascertained by going from house to house how many had once named the name of Christ. These had been brought together. Mutual confessions had been made. Old covenants had been renewed. Regular meetings during the week had been established. Occasional preaching for the Sabbath had been secured. A Sunday-school had been organized, and it was but a little time before the habits of the neighborhood were revolutionized.

How many times he set such a train of influences working only God knows. This incident had altogether dropped from his mind till some unknown friend put it into a tract for circulation and accidentally the tract fell under his eye only three or four years before he died.

In the summer of 1851 he comes East again, to visit his aged mother, and in the autumn he is sent to Cleveland, Ohio, a city in which some of his most effective work was done. This arrangement was effected through his old pastor, Rev. J. Hyatt Smith, at this date prosecuting a most successful ministry in Cleveland. Inclined always to self-depreciation, Uncle John seems apprehensive that his style of labor will not be liked among city circles and cultivated folks.

He imagines the backwoods his sphere. He regrets that he was not left there, and makes the new depart-. ure with earnest prayers for help. Soon, however, his letters undergo a change. They take on a more cheerful tone. He finds that human nature is much the same, whether in a log-cabin of one room or a brownstone front on the avenue. Everywhere he is given the most cordial welcome. His books sell as he has never seen them sell before. The churches make most generous collections for the Society, the Rev. Mr. Smith's contributing six hundred dollars in two days. Nor do they in giving to the service overlook the servant's wants. Thus modestly he mentions a timely gift: "While writing the other evening a gentleman called with a bundle, containing a note from some unknown friend, a very handsome overcoat, and a pair of gloves. The coat is much too fine and fashionable for me, but the note says that I must wear it, so what else can I do?" We shall not misjudge the good man if we suppose that in the new garment he felt more comfortable in going from house to house than in the old one, which had done prairie service. While his tastes were plain, and fashions of little consequence, he liked to be respectably attired, especially where a rusty garb might excite prejudice and impair his usefulness.

More gratifying to him, however, than personal attentions and generous collections, or large sales, was the spiritual quickening which was enjoyed. The details are but meagrely given, the most that he records being in these lines: "I visit frequently forty families a day, have a meeting somewhere every night, and speak to three Sunday-schools where practicable every Lord's day. I have conversed with over three thousand people during the last three months on the subject of personal religion, and feel that for this city a wonderful blessing is in store."

Happily the facts and incidents of that memorable winter can, in part at least, be furnished by those who moved amid them, some of whom during it felt the Spirit's touch unto eternal life. What one man did— rather what God through him did—let these in their own way tell.

Rev. George M. Stone, D.D., of Tarrytown, N.Y., thus writes: "My first acquaintance with Uncle John was in Cleveland, Ohio, in the year 1852. He was visiting from house to house, and in that portion of the city a remarkable religious interest was soon manifest. I was then an unconverted young man about eighteen years of age, and engaged in a printing office. A. companion in the office, who had heard of the eloquence of Rev. J. Hyatt Smith, invited me to accompany him one evening to the lecture-room of his church, where meetings were being held. I went, and was interested in the preaching. As I arose to pass out, after the service, I was approached by a person, then a stranger, who asked with mingled earnestness and kindness if I loved the Lord Jesus Christ. He took my hand at the same time, and held it firmly. I can never forget the intense sincerity of that first interview. I felt in a moment that I had never before met

a man who possessed such a transcendent consciousness of divine things. That stranger was John E. Vassar, and from that hour convictions began to stir my
heart which in time the Holy Spirit used to lead me to
Christ.

"He assisted me in religious meetings subsequently
at Danbury, Conn., and in visitations in Milwaukee,
Wisconsin. In this association with him his experience
seemed to be a perpetual summer of Christian love."

Hear again his friend Rev. J. Hyatt Smith: "On his
way to Illinois as a colporteur of the American Tract
Society, he surprised me by calling at my house one
day. I urged him to remain a while. He refused, and
left that same night on a steamer for Detroit. The boat
was so crowded that I was afraid to have him go on
board. I remember his look as he replied, 'I rejoice
that so many are going. I shall have a blessed time
working for souls.' Away he went on an overloaded
steamer in a stormy night, and I went to my home
praying for him.

"Through my letters to the Society he was afterward transferred to Cleveland, and remained there six
months. The work that he wrought for the Master in
my church, to say nothing of the abundant and effective labors outside of my parish, God alone may estimate. I could fill pages with incidents, if the limits of
this volume would permit.

"One day Brother Vassar came to me and said, 'Tomorrow I am going through Dives Street (Euclid
Street), and I want you to pray for me.' I promised

him I would, and requested him to report to me the results of his first day's visit to the houses of wealth on that beautiful avenue. I give a report of his visit to the first house on his journey. At the door of the stately dwelling he met the lady of the house. 'What do you want, sir?' she asked, as he approached her. He replied, 'I am a colporteur for the Tract Society, and' –pointing to his basket of books— 'I am selling these.' 'We have a library,' was her reply. 'I don't doubt it,' said Brother Vassar, glancing at the building; ' but,' he continued, nothing daunted by the rather sharp response of the lady, 'the truth is I am legs for Bunyan, Baxter, Flavel, and others. They are all in the basket there.' The lady, evidently struck with the appearance of the man and the quaintness of his address, asked him into the parlor. Having stormed and carried the house, he began an assault upon the castle of the heart. 'I am not only a seller of books, but I am anxious to know if you love Jesus,' said John. 'I am a member of the church,' the woman replied. 'So am I,' said Brother Vassar, 'but I fear that God will not take our church records. He counts the names recorded in the Lamb's Book of Life.' The attack was fairly commenced, and the arrows of love flew thick and fast. Heart Castle surrendered; the lady with tears exclaimed, 'I know it is not enough to belong to a church. You talk like my dear mother. Yes, I trust I do love Jesus.' 'Bless the Lord,' said John, 'that makes us brother and sister. If you love the Saviour, and I see you do, would

5

you not like a season of prayer?' She replied, 'I would be glad to have you pray.' They knelt side by side, and John poured out his soul in supplication. At the close of the prayer the lady asked, 'What is the price of your books?' 'Which one?' said Brother Vassar. *'All of them,'* was her answer. The calculation was made; then calling a servant she bade him carry them to the library, paid Brother Vassar for them, gave him something for himself, and with tears in her eyes begged him to forgive her manner at the door. 'Don't mention it, my sister,' said Brother Vassar, 'you know what our blessed Master had to bear.'

"His manner in the prayer-meeting, as I remember it in those distant days, and that which I have seen in his later life, was in my judgment much the same. I do not think his character had those stages of growth which mark most Christian men. In Christ Jesus he seemed to have been born a man of full stature. It is said of the river Jordan that, unlike most streams, it does not start with small springs and receive the contributions of rivulets by the way, so attaining fulness, but bursts forth from one vast source, a river rolling to the sea.

"I never met his like in all the varied labors of a saint. He was a master in all the sword exercise of God's Word."

With this Cleveland campaign, service in what might be called the Department of the West for a season ended. Years afterward he was again on some of these old camp-grounds.

CHAPTER V.

OFF ON FURLOUGH.

> "Rest is not quitting
> The busy career;
> Rest is the fitting
> Of self to its sphere."

THE summer of 1852 found Uncle John again in his old home. His mother had gone far beyond her three score and ten years, and growing feebleness indicated that the end was not far away. The only child remaining with her was a daughter who from girlhood had been frail. It became a question whether duty did not require him to stay where he could smooth the last few months of a parent whose devotion to her children had been unsurpassed. Satisfied that maternal claims were for the present paramount, he dissolved his connection with the Tract Society, and waited tenderly on the failing steps of the mother till October, when he laid her down in hope by the good father's side.

Friends in Poughkeepsie now insisted that there was work enough for him at home, and especially in the temperance line. In many places the so-called "Carson League" had been organized, the chief object of which was to suppress the unlicensed sale of intoxicating drink. This Society pressed him to become its agent in Dutchess County, to bring to justice offenders against law. It is needless to remark that this was vastly less congenial employment than telling "the old, old story of Jesus and his love." But the evil to be fought was a crying one, and what right had any child of God to decline a service simply because it was disagreeable? He would be withstanding sin and Satan still. So he grappled with the whiskey power, and it never found in that region a foe who dealt it heavier blows, or one whom it was so difficult to scare or beat. As religiously as he ever went to his closet to pray he ferreted out law-breakers in saloons, and groceries, and taverns, and groggeries, nor rested till a number were inside of prison bars instead of liquor bars, and dozens more, alarmed, gave up the illicit trade. As might be expected, "certain lewd fellows of the baser sort" cursed and threatened and reviled. They hung him in effigy in front of the County Court House with the inscription, "This is John Vassar and the Maine Law." They prosecuted him in court on a charge of assault and battery because one day, in an earnest argument, he held a man for a moment by the arm, when he was about to turn away. They followed him on the streets in hooting rabbles. His life was more than once in jeopardy. One of these attempts to frighten, if not to injure him, let one who witnessed it describe—L. T. Perkins, Esq., of Brooklyn, N. Y., then a Poughkeepsie boy.

"One afternoon he came up Market Street to Main, and up Main to the Gregory House, followed by some two hundred angry men, many of them carrying clubs and threatening his life. He passed through the hotel by a back way, and came down Mill Street to our church, where the usual prayer-meeting was about to begin. I shall never forget the burning enthusiasm of the man as he spoke that night, or the fervor of his prayer. After the meeting I wanted to go home with him, being fearful that he might be harmed. I know it was absurd to think that my five-foot and hundred-pound body could have done much toward protecting him, but I loved him, and so I wished to go along. As we were coming up the basement steps, our pastor, Rev. Thomas Goodwin, said, 'Here, Brother Vassar, take this cane of mine; I can get along without it, and some of these men may be lurking along the streets and may fall on you.' Uncle John just braced himself back, held up both hands, and said, 'Brother Goodwin, the Lord has given me these hands for weapons, and they are all I need. If my Master wants John Vassar to-night, nothing can save him. If He does not, all these men combined can't hurt him."

For two years he thus pushed this work, during which time he saw his steadfast friend, the late George W. Sterling, sent to the State Legislature from the Pough-keepsie district, on a straight-out temperance ticket, and other triumphs won neither few nor small. Concerning these days this is about all the record we have from his own hand: "I look back with wonder to see how much the Lord has brought me through. Blessed be His holy name. I have visited the nineteen towns of the county, and some of them twice over. I have walked on an average twenty miles a day, and spoken publicly about every night. I believe some good has been done, but I take to myself no praise. I am an unprofitable servant anywhere, and far too little concerned for any good cause."

Toward the close of these labors—in December, 1854—he was married to Miss Harriet M. Brownson, formerly of Monticello, Sullivan County, N. Y., but at the date of the marriage a very active member of the Poughkeepsie church. In entering into this new relation it was understood that the remainder of his life was to be devoted to evangelistic labor, and that this labor would be likely to make of him literally a pilgrim and stranger, having no continuing city, no permanent or settled home. Animated by much of his spirit, the wife sought in nowise to hold him back, but at the first, as ever afterward, consented readily to such separations as long absences required, and such an increase of care and duty as they might bring. Bible work, in his native county, claimed his attention for six months or more. The object in securing him was to effect if possible an entrance into every house of the county, and the putting of a copy of God's Word in every home where it was not found. So thorough a canvass of that field no one man has ever made. From the shanties of the coal-burners on Fishkill Mountains, to the mansions of the wealthiest in the towns he went, and in almost every instance was well received. A few, irritated by his recent temperance work, shut their doors in his face, but several such were melted when he promptly knelt down upon the stoop, and tenderly prayed that in turning him away they might not turn away his Lord. For Romanists who would receive no other, the Douay version was carried, and so in the autumn he was able to report that there were few families in all the district in which the Scriptures could not be seen.

The wide acquaintance thus acquired led the Dutchess Baptist Association to recognize in him the man above all others to undertake mission work within their bounds. This body embraced some twenty or more churches, and amid these for seven or eight years he now moved, aiding by prayer and exhortation in extra meetings, and especially in visiting from house to house. Here it was that he first took on himself the title of "Shepherd's dog," a title which thereafter clung to him, and by which he was almost as well known as "Uncle John." It originated in the fact that he always and everywhere refused to be considered a preacher, declaring that it was his office simply to go around and seek out, and bring under the minister's notice, anxious and troubled souls. These years were years of growth such as his own denomination had not known through that region for a long while, and never since has seen. The revival spirit went from church to church. Drowsy Christians started up where he came, as sleeping soldiers at bugle call. Formal professors thawed out into a spring-time of devotion as frozen clods thaw out when April winds breathe across the fields. Hundreds bowed as penitent sinners at the Saviour's feet, and rose to walk in newness of life with their risen Lord.

Many who labored with him in these seasons have passed on with their brother toiler, and entered into rest. Others remain. Let them add their testimony here.

Rev. W. O. Holman, of Bunker Hill Church, Boston, writes: "I was studying for the ministry in the city of New York, and was supplying the Baptist church in Amenia, twenty-five miles east of Poughkeepsie, a church which was at the time pastorless, when our acquaintance began. A revival had broken out in our meetings, and Uncle John was soon on hand. One Sunday, while I was preaching, a short, thick-set man, with a genial countenance, came in. He took a seat near the pulpit, and putting his eyes intently on me kept his lips moving, as if in assent or prayer. At the close of the service he grasped my hand, and was so hearty and cordial and enthusiastic that I was almost repelled. He interested me nevertheless, and we were soon the best of friends. Blessed be God for the hour that brought us together. I have known many a good man after the flesh, but never another such as he.

"Together we travelled from house to house, over hill and dale, through cold and snow, rain and sunshine, seeking for sinners to lead to Christ. Never shall I forget his apt, earnest, pointed appeals. The fruits of that meeting were glorious. Old feuds among believers were healed, and from fifty to seventy souls converted to the Lord. A year or more afterward I was ordained and settled at Poughkeepsie, and so became the pastor of Uncle John. There we worked together in a most blessed season in the spring of 1858. On a single Sabbath I was privileged to give the hand of fellowship to sixty-three new believers, many of whom still survive, and some of whom were permitted to drop the tear of affection over one who helped guide their returning feet to the Shepherd and Bishop of souls.

"The next August we went to Beekman, where there was a little feeble church, for a four days' meeting. It was right in harvest-time, but the people flocked together, and the literal harvest was nothing alongside the harvest of souls which there was gathered in. The four days' service ran into four weeks, and it really seemed as if Uncle John's heart and head were in heaven, while his feet yet trod the earth. That community will tell of his toils and travels, during those weeks, forever.

"Thence we went to Fishkill Plains and Shenandoah, and oh! the sweet wonders of redeeming grace that were displayed. Uncle John seemed divinely anointed. If ever soul revelled in the love of Christ, he did. He testified to every one who would listen by day, and then far into the night he would wrestle for anxious souls. Winter after winter in Poughkeepsie, during my five years' pastorate, he would come home long enough to labor for a while. God uniformly gave

His blessing, and the precious revivals of those early years are hallowed in my heart forever. Oh for one more hour with the dear old man, one more prayer together, one more exhortation, one Scripture exposition such as he used to give; but alas! we shall see his face and hear his voice no more."

Rev. J. Donnelly, of Ionia, Michican, says: "In August of 1858 Uncle John came out to Beekman, where I, then a student at Hamilton was supplying the church. I shall never forget the day he came to my study. I was busy writing out a sermon for Sunday, and was about half done, when a rap at my door brought him in. Greetings were soon exchanged, a season of prayer followed, and in thirty minutes from the time he entered we were out calling and at missionary work. I did not see how I could go, at first, and leave my sermon unfinished. But I went. That sermon was never finished. Before Sunday came, ay, before the first night, there were anxious souls inquiring after Christ, and my subject had to be changed. Over forty-five persons, as the result of the work thus begun, were added to the church, and of the human agencies employed Uncle John must be accounted first. For what I then and there learned, for the breaking-in I received in the matter of dealing with souls, I have thanked John Vassar since a thousand times. During this revival I was much with him, and can testify that the last thing before his eyes closed was prayer, and the first when his eyes opened. After an experience of twenty years I am free to say that I never knew a man who prayed so much, and I never knew a man who lived so constantly in the sunshine of a Saviour's presence and love. If ever a man lived Christ, it was John E. Vassar."

Of these same meetings Rev. J. L. Benedict, of White Plains, N. Y., a college classmate of Mr. Donnelly, gives this account: "On entering the village of Beekman on a visit to my friend, who was supplying the little church there, I did not know just where to find him; so, accosting a man who was nearing me and walking very fast, I inquired. The stranger thus addressed pointed out the place, and in the next breath said, "Are you a Christian, my young friend?" I answered that I hoped I was. A few more words passed, and then he went on, remarking that he was 'in a hurry to look up some sheep.' After greeting my fellow student, and being introduced to the family in which he made his home, I remarked that I had just met a crazy man up the road in search of some sheep. The whole group laughed outright, and my friend said, 'Why, that was John Vassar, our county missionary; and the sheep that he is in search of are the Lord's.' A few days afterward Uncle John wished me to accompany him to the old Fishkill church, a few miles below, where the venerable Elder Robinson had preached for many years. This aged minister was not friendly to protracted meetings, yet he and his church had confidence in Uncle John, and readily consented to open their house of worship for a week. The very first evening five young men rose for prayer, and within a month between thirty and forty made a public profession of their faith. One day I accompanied Uncle John in his visits, and we called at the house of Mr. S., where there were several young people, unconverted then. On our approach they ran into another room to get out of the way. He saw the movement, and went straight in where they were. Then, with all the tender sympathy of his great heart, he entreated them to yield to Christ, and falling on his knees pleaded for them separately each by name. Before we left the house they were in tears, and were praying for themselves. They all became living witnesses for Christ. During the course of the day we stopped under the shade of a large oak to rest, and while stopping there I took occasion to ask him if he always thus followed up those who sought to avoid him. He replied that he did not, that ordinarily it might irritate them, but that in cases where he believed the Spirit of God was working, and especially in revival seasons, he would so hunt them up.

"To make more clear his meaning he told me of an instance which occurred not long before, but charged me never to repeat it publicly, lest it should excite a laugh and divert attention from more serious concerns. Somewhere in 'a meeting he had met a young man troubled evidently about his salvation, and apparently more than half persuaded to settle the conflict by out-and-out committal of himself to the Lord. One day Uncle John felt the impression very strong that he ought to go and see this wavering soul. It was nearly noon, and the men on the farm were coming in from the field. All gathered around the table for dinner save the one that it was desired to reach. The father said that the son would probably be in presently, but he did not come. Uncle John feared that he was keeping out of the way purposely, and determined to go out and look him up. Through all the out-buildings he searched and called, but without success, and was about to give up the quest when he chanced to spy the door of a corn-crib open, and entering it, in a large hogshead he found the young man concealed. Climbing right over into it by the trembling, confounded, humiliated sinner's side, he began to talk and pray, and there the penitent settled the question to be forever the Lord's. Afterward he confessed to Uncle John that when he saw him hunting around he took a sort of malicious satisfaction in thinking he had evaded him. The devil was making his last effort to retain in his clutch a troubled soul. But when discovery came, then over the fugitive crept such a sense of shame, and meanness, and foolishness, and wickedness, as made him loathe himself, and prepared him to fall as a weak and guilty thing into the Saviour's arms. Very distinctly Uncle John affirmed that it would not answer to so treat every case, and very solemnly he adjured me as a young preacher never to tell anything in preaching that would make men see me when they ought to see Christ, or think of my adroitness or shrewdness when they ought to be thinking of His love and grace. Then, having thus counselled me, he

6*

bowed under that grand old oak and wrestled for a blessing as once in the past Jacob did.

"More than twenty years have passed since I spent those three happy weeks with John E. Vassar, but I learned more practical theology, more about the working of God's Spirit on the hearts of men, more about the way to deal with the impenitent or awakened, than in any like period of all my life. The man who could convert a hogshead into a Bethel was of the right stamp for a country missionary, and must have many imitators if the wanderers are to be brought nigh.'"

An aged woman, Mrs. A. B. Minor, of New Haven County, Conn., contributes these items, bringing out several characteristics of the man.

"One winter, when Mr. Vassar was assisting his nephew, then pastor at Amenia, N. Y., he came over to Sharon, Conn., not more than half a dozen miles away, where was then my home. For my unconverted son, about twenty years of age, he at once became interested, facing him with this question soon as they met, 'Tell me, G., do you love the Lord Jesus?' From that interview my child dated his hope. He has been for eleven years now in the heavenly home, and I think with what joy he must have given welcome to the man who did so much to guide him there.

"There was another man in the neighborhood far from righteousness. Mr. Vassar went over to his house, and taking up a little child belonging there he said, 'I love these little ones, and want their parents to bring them up for God.' The stout-hearted father melted right down, and soon in our meetings his voice was leading us in prayer.

"Another aged man, very moral and upright, but long oppressed with the fear that he had been given over by God, was, under Mr. Vassar's labors, led out into the light, and brought where he could praise and pray. So God blessed his efforts, and when I think of those days in '58 and '59, and '60, and how the dear young people, as well as those older, were drawn toward him, and not only toward him, but to that Saviour whom he served, I bless God for ever having known him, and for the sweet remembrances that come rising up."

Rev. G. F. Hendrickson, of Fairview, N. J., sends these recollections: "A week after accepting the pastoral care of the South Dover Church, in the spring of 1857, Uncle John as county missionary came upon that field. At once our meetings began to fill up, for he would pass no one without inviting him to the house of God. Many who rarely if ever attended church were through his efforts brought there, and a dozen or fifteen found Christ, some of whom are with him on the other side of time and death today. During these labors Uncle John was taken very ill; and it fell to my lot to nurse and wait upon him; and never did I see such faith and trust. Again and again he would say to us when recovery seemed improbable, 'I shall not die, but live to declare God's salvation.' Often that sick-room was like the gate of heaven.

"Two years later he again aided me in what was

the most powerful revival that church has ever known. Among ministers and members of our churches all through that region his memory will long abide a precious and sacred trust."

Mrs. A. E. Beckwith, of Stissing, N. Y., gives these recollections and impressions of the period lying between 1854 and 1862: "It was a great pleasure to see Uncle John come into our home, for he always brought so much of heaven along. The all-absorbing passion of his soul was love to God and the perishing around him. In the winter of 1857-58 he began visiting in our neighborhood, and evening meetings at the school-house were begun. So intense was the interest developed that the services had to be removed to the church. The whole town of Stanford was aroused, and nearly two hundred are believed to have turned to God. Later, while Dr. Holman served as pastor, and especially in 1860 or 1861, a powerful religious awakening followed his visits and the preaching of the Word. He would take different localities day after day, appointing in each a meeting for the afternoon. One day—perhaps at one or two o'clock—he came hurrying into our house, asking for something to eat. His boots were all soaked with snow water, and he had eaten nothing so far that day. He had fasted till he could get an assurance of a blessing on the labor undertaken, and now it had been given. In these efforts of his he would kneel and pray with the anxious anywhere he found them, in the barn, the field, even in the snow along the road."

Mrs. E. A. Ketcham, of Dover Plains, N. Y., says: "The world has sustained a loss in his removal. The story of his life and labors, if *it could be written*, would prove a blessing to thousands. I remember with joy and thankfulness his labors in our church at different times. His last visit especially we all recall. He stopped at my son's to dinner, and two little prayer-meetings were held in that single hour."

Uncle John's true yoke-fellow during this Dutchess County work was Rev. C. B. Post, of Dover Plains. With the exception possibly of his own pastor, and the compiler of this book, no other minister knew him during those years so well. He no longer shares in the struggles and victories of Christ's militant Church, but Mrs. Post from her home near the "Golden Gate," in the far West, sends these memorials of those years:

"It is nearly twenty-four years since he first came to our house, and during the seven years followng he and my husband labored together weeks and months in our own or other towns. Brother Vassar would commonly go first, talking and praying with the people; and when he saw the mercy-cloud beginning to gather, he would send for Mr. Post, saying, 'Come, bishop, the Lord wants you to feed the sheep that He shall use me to bring together.'

"One winter, when coming to labor with our own church, a heavy snow-storm set in. It continued till the roads were blocked. In this condition they kept for several days. The people could not get out, and meetings were not to be thought of. But he could not be snow-bound. He would flounder through the drifts somehow, often kneeling in them to thank God for mercies granted or plead with God for mercies needed.

"Once when talking with our Sunday-school about the death of his little son he said, 'When I laid Johnny down out of my arms into the arms of the dear Saviour, this world and I forever parted company.' We all believed that utterance was true, and felt persuaded that the partnership there and thus dissolved had never since been renewed.

"He once gave me an idea never to be forgotten. Something was being said about ill-treatment which he had encountered, on a certain visit. He quickly replied, 'A sinner cannot abuse old John Vassar. The poor lost soul! oh, how I love him!'

"A marked trait in his character was his love for God's ministers. No unjust or severe criticism ever escaped his lips. They were the Lord's chosen messengers, and he loved them for the Master's sake. The affection between Mr. Post and him was mutual and very strong. It is no less strong now that they see the King in His beauty, and are forever with the Lord."

Of this same period Mrs. Sarah L. Lyon, Poughkeepsie, tells: "It was in the early part of March, 1860 that this man of God was directed to my father's house. The winter had been unusually severe, so that the drifts of snow yet lay over the fences, and the road leading up over the hill to our home was fairly blocked. We were therefore surprised to see a stranger on foot pushing along it, and finally making for our door. As he came nearer he was recognized as John Vassar, of temperance renown. To my mother he was a welcome visitor, but not to me. I would have escaped the interview but for the importunity of my mother, who said, 'Stay and listen to a man who has travelled through this snow knee-deep to do us good.' I tried to repulse him when he began to plead with me, by talking of universal salvation, which in my impenitence I had tried to find safety in; but his clear reasoning quickly swept such arguments away. Then he asked us to kneel while he poured out his soul in prayer. And such a prayer we never heard. We were all melted down. His visit was short, but it was wonderful. Three of our names were added to the list that he called his 'dear children in Christ Jesus,' and a fire of sacred love was kindled in our hearts, never, we trust, to go out. The home-roof of my childhood was long since exchanged for another, to which I have ever esteemed it an honor to give him welcome, and under which children now gather who have been taught to rise up and call him blessed.

"The benediction was not confined to our household. A revival in the neighborhood broke out, which spread wide, and proved lasting; and many, I believe, will, to and through eternity, sing love's redeeming song from the work then and there done by this good man."

Another says: "I cannot now name the date, but about twenty years ago Mr. S. was drawing a load along the road when he met a stranger, who stopped and said, ' What may I call your name, sir?' The one addressed replied, 'My name is S.' 'Ah, you are a deacon in the church here, are you not?' was the response. 'I am, sir,' was the answer. 'Well, deacon,' said the stranger, 'my name is Vassar—John Vassar; now, is your wife a Christian?' 'I am sorry to say that she is not.' 'Have you any objection to my calling and conversing with your family?' 'Not the least, not the least.' 'God bless you, Brother S. Good morning.' Uncle John passed along, and the deacon went on and turned into a field with his load. He had not gone more than thirty rods when the thought came to him, 'How is this? Here is a stranger more concerned for the salvation of my household than I am. This is not right. This won't do.' Mr. S. jumped off his load, unhitched the horses from the sled, tied them, and started for the house. He arrived just in time to hear the prayer. That load was not moved again for six weeks. Mrs. S. was converted, and forty-two others united with the Kent and East Fishkill Church."

For obvious reasons the following touching statement is given without its author's name:

"Uncle John came to my father's house for the first time more than a quarter of a century ago. My father was at that time an inebriate, and our home was suffering under the blight of rum. His coming was the beginning of better days. It resulted in the conversion of the father and all seven of us children. Two of the children are now in the ministry, two others, together with the parents, have died in hope, and we are waiting for a happy family reunion on the river's other side.

"Fifteen years later, in company with my brother, he visited the same house, and that interview resulted in the salvation of the man and his wife then living there."

Of these days an army friend has this to say: "He was never happier in his life, he has told me, than when wading through the snowdrifts from farm to farm in old Dutchess County.

"How vividly I recall the play of countenance, the animation of voice, the gesture with which, night after night, with all the camp around us asleep, he poured out the narrative, while I lent him a charmed ear, and laughed and cried together.

"He had scores of stories to tell. One of his experiences during this period, as he related it, I vividly remember. I will give only its main features, not attempting to repeat his words.

"He went to one place which had long been under the blight of spiritual declension, and where among the youth of the community there was not a single professing Christian. He was informed that the leading spirit in the social life of the place was a young woman— that her influence was commanding, and that it was used against religion. If she could be won to Christ, a great point would be gained. So Uncle John went to see her first. As soon as she understood the object of his visit, she rudely refused to listen to him, and bade him begone forthwith without another word. He left her, and went calling elsewhere. And presently about everybody he met treated him coldly. At a number of houses he was denied admission, in one instance with violent words. He did not know what to make of it. But the explanation soon came out. The young woman he had first visited, in her extreme anger at him, had declared that he had offered her an insult, and the falsehood was going the rounds, and was everywhere ahead of him.

"This fact, he said when he first discovered it, seemed to him the most mysterious providence he had ever heard of. 'O Lord, what does it mean?' he cried in dismay. His work was completely blocked. There was no help for it; and he had to go. Wondering greatly, but submitting, he went to another field some distance away, and began laboring there. He had been there awhile, and was seeing hopeful signs of good, when one evening as he was holding a meeting in a schoolhouse, he heard a large, heavily-loaded sleigh drive up and stop at the door. When the door was opened, there appeared a party of some twenty young people, with the young woman before mentioned at their head. Mr. Vassar's first thought was that they had come to mob him or do him harm of some sort. They came in, the whole company, all strangers, and the silence that followed was broken by the young woman standing forth and saying, in a trembling voice, 'Mr. Vassar, I have brought these friends of mine with me to hear me ask your forgiveness for the great wrong I did you when you were in our place. Telling that lie was the meanest thing I ever did. That I could tell it, and that I felt like telling it, for such a cause, showed me as I never saw it before, the wickedness of my heart—my state as a sinner. It has led me, I trust, to ask God's forgiveness, and I hope that for Christ's sake he has heard my prayer. Will you forgive me, too?' " To all these memories of twenty years ago we might add dozens treasured up in our own mind, for from 1856 to 1862 we labored together in full half the towns of the county we called home. Although settled in the pastorate at Amenia, we went as other ministers around did at that time, to help in neighboring churches as occasion might require. Again and again in these campaigns we have known him to walk twenty miles in a single day, looking up wanderers or seekers, and then come into the evening service showing no sign of weariness in motion, or look, or voice.

Once in trudging along in a snowy road he was overtaken by a gentleman in a sleigh, who was personally a very estimable man, but not a Christian. He knew Uncle John by sight, and like many others did not admire him, but rather regarded him as fanatical or half insane. Whether to ask him to ride or not was the question in his mind. Courtesy said "Yes;" prejudice said "No." Courtesy carried the day, however, and the invitation was given. An opportunity like that never was allowed to slip. The ride was not accounted of so much consequence, but there would be such a chance to press home truth as the Master had that day at the well of Jacob. It was embraced to the uttermost, and one man heard that hour salvation urged as he certainly never had heard it urged before. What the immediate effect was is not known, but a few months later this wayside hearer, then in the very prime of life, came to know experimentally the meaning of those words, If any man be in Christ he is a new creature." Immediately after old things had passed away the two men met at church, and, deeply moved, clasped hands as brothers beloved in the Lord. The circumstances must be very, very peculiar if they ever hindered him from pressing religion on the mind. He was not indelicate, or rude, or blustering in approaching men, but he remembered that one divinely inspired had said, "In season, *out of season,* reprove, rebuke, exhort," and so he could not stand "on the proprieties," as many do. Near Fishkill he once made a call that seemed at first inopportune. A young man had just entered the house, who was soon to be married to an excellent Christian daughter in the home. The prospective husband claimed no hope in the Saviour. Either accidentally or purposely, we know not which, Uncle John was shown into the room where the parties were. He took in the situation at a glance, but, not in the least disconcerted, pressed on one of his two hearers the claims of God, and finding him more than half persuaded to accept of Christ, he closed the interview by proposing that the lady should herself then and there kneel and present the case of her friend to God. For a moment maidenly delicacy led her to hesitate; then seeing his evident concern they all bowed together, and she pleaded for the salvation of the man with whom she was to walk the pathway of life. He was soon a partaker of her faith and trust, and stood beside her a fellow-laborer in the Church of Christ.

One day, while walking from Poughkeepsie to Pleasant Valley, he overtook a man driving an ox-team along the road. Walking on together in conversation it was but a minute or two before the Name that is above every name was on the lips of Uncle John, and the subject ever uppermost was broached. With the utmost frankness, and with a trembling voice, the man declared that for weeks he had been secretly trying to grope his way to God. He had said nothing to any one, and no one had said anything to him. All was uncertainty with him and gloom. That Saviour who " must needs go through Samaria" so long ago, because there was a lost soul waiting to hear words of life, sent the right man to this inquiring soul that day. Uncle John knew how to meet a case like that. His words fitted that penitent's wants as the notch in the arrow is fitted to the string of the archer's bow. The mode of a sinner's acceptance was seen that very hour. By the roadside they knelt in prayer together, and then they parted, this convert, like one in the olden time, going on his way rejoicing.

Hardly had they separated before Uncle John saw a man ploughing in a field some distance from the highway. All aglow with the recent interview the ques-

7*

tion started, "May I not find yonder another such a case? Who knows?" Across the lot he hurried, and strange as it may seem, he did find another soul anxious and ready to accept of Christ. In the freshly turned furrows the two knelt, and either then or very soon afterward the peace of God entered this heart too.

In this town of Pleasant Valley he saw some wonderful triumphs of redeeming love. His old friend, Rev. B. F. Wile, of the Presbyterian Church, often had him, for a week or two, when he was not otherwise engaged, to aid him in some of those times of ingathering which that church so signally enjoyed.

In the little Baptist church at Salt Point, in the same town, there were in those far-off years seasons of great-refreshing. Amid them some who are with their Lord now, and some who on earth are useful still, started for the kingdom and the crown.

In the autumn of 1862 the section of country around Carmel, Putnam County, N. Y., enjoyed Uncle John's labors for some weeks, a very minute and interesting account of which has been furnished by Rev. J. J. Townsend, now of Chester, Vermont, at that time studying for the ministry, but at home on a visit. Only some extracts from it can be given.

"The evening following Uncle John's arrival in the neighborhood, I had an engagement to lecture in the Nichols school-house, and he met me there. After my little talk he followed in exhortation and prayer. At the close of the service he said, 'You are just the young man I am looking for. Come with me.' The Master has work for you.'

"The next night we took another neighborhood, he first thoroughly canvassing it by day. The house was crowded. I preached, and he followed in an exhortation the most solemn and subduing I ever heard. The Master was there, and sinners were crying for salvation before the meeting closed.

"There were eight of these school-districts within the bounds of the Carmel church. From one to another of these we went, and he from house to house. God triumphed gloriously. The whole field glowed with religious life. The meetings grew so large that they had to be carried to the church. Pastor Clapp then supervised, or, as Uncle John said, became 'Major-General.'

"For three months we were together thus by day and night. One day, while out on our rounds, we saw a man in the field husking corn. Uncle John said, 'Let us kneel down here and pray, and then go after him.' We did so. Soon as we began to talk with him we found out that he was a man at whose house we had just called. He had a wife and three children, and none of them entertained a hope of pardoned sin. He was invited first to attend the meeting. He refused flatly, declared he was a Universalist, but admitted that he never prayed. Then Uncle John poured out upon him all the truth of God. I never saw him more valiant for his Master, and think it was one of his grandest hours. With tears streaming down his cheeks the man said, 'Pray for me,' and down among the stalks we all three bowed, and all three prayed. He and three others from his family were soon in the kingdom.

"This scene is one of many. Strong oaks on every hand bowed before the mighty on-movings of God's all-conquering grace.

"We one day met a man on the road, resting his team, who, on being approached, loudly avowed himself an infidel. So tremendous was the pressure under which Uncle John put him that in five minutes, with wonder and penitence written on his face, he gladly bowed to have prayer offered in his behalf, and on arising and parting he said, 'I need this Saviour, and will seek him.'

"One evening, as we were going into meeting, we met a gentleman near the door. Uncle John addressed him courteously, and said, 'My dear friend, do you love Jesus?' Said the gentleman, 'I do not know that that concerns you, sir.' 'Oh, yes, it does,' said Uncle John; 'in these days of rebellion does it not concern every citizen as to which side every other citizen may take? How much more when a world is in rebellion against God should we be concerned to know who is on the Lord's side.' The man's lips were sealed. Before the meeting was over he rose and asked the prayers of God's people. And thus it was in every case. I certainly saw him personally address hundreds, and in no solitary instance was he repulsed.

'For myself I can say that this three months' tuition in the school of Christ, with John Vassar as tutor, has been worth more to me in winning souls than any like period of my life. His religion was not that of sentiment, but a soul-subduing force, fed at the fountain of almighty and undecaying promise, and it helped me to heights before unknown.

"As we parted, he to return to his home, and I to go back to Hamilton, after a season of delightful prayer he said, 'Good-by; God bless you. Keep looking up, my boy, keep looking up.'

"When John Vassar was removed from the high places of the field, truly a great man had fallen in Israel. He to whom the King holds out the sceptre, as with him, is an irreparable loss to any church, any community, or any age."

Now, what do all these toils and triumphs represent? They represent homes made happier; hearts blessed with a heavenly peace; the wicked turned into penitents; sick-beds solaced with comforts such as earth is powerless to give; graves that had otherwise been hopeless bordered with a brighter than noonday light; a stubborn, unbelieving world yielding converts to the Church; a quickened Church shedding on the world a brightness like that of the resurrection morning.

Conversion must be recognized as a constituent power of history. That deep sorrow for sin, that clear and shining sense of God's forgiveness, that unearthly peace and joy, that glowing love for Christ and for His saints, that glad hope of heaven, that desire to do others good which we call "experience" and the world calls "delusion," all lay at the bottom of that man's life who rang out the old ideas of Greece and Rome, and rang in a new age; they all lay at the bottom of that man's life who lifted his hand in the face of papal Europe and gave the signal for its disruption; they all lay at the bottom of that man's life who in a corrupt nation and a degenerating Church more than a century ago cried, "The world is my parish," and went out to awaken it. And revivals, what are they but renewals of the apostolic age? Even among good men there is a tendency to let the heavenly fire die out—to let the immortal vitality and infinite resources of our holy religion go unfelt and unseen. Christ's churches forget that they are to subdue the world, and quietly settle into their quarters, and then God sends some man with clarion call to bid the slumbering host bestir itself. Doubtless there will be in all such awakenings some extravagances. This world is full of weak, ill-balanced, blundering folks. Either they must go unsaved, or else a miracle more stupendous than was ever wrought must keep them from acting extravagantly. The second supposition is improbable. The first may God avert. The composure of death is worse than the exuberance of life. And we may be sure that without these arousings that old Christianity which gave the world apostles, and missionaries, and martyrs, will be replaced by another which will give it only formal church-goers.

Nor is it any argument against such seasons of quickening as the few last pages have been dealing with, that much of their early promise seems to be blasted, and drop fruitlessly away. That is always so with the literal bud and bloom which May days bring. Multitudes of people are naturally unstable, and their instability will be likely to affect the religious life more or less. We question whether there is any ground for the prevalent idea that persons converted in revivals are less likely to "hold out," or "hold on." That will depend on what they have to "hold on" to. If it is nothing but a mere stir of the sensibilities, of course they will drop away. A very sober Christian scholar says, "Let the spring come, though it bring weeds, and let us neither nurse the weeds nor frost-bite the wheat in our impatience to keep them down." It might be added, moreover, that much which accompanies a revival of religion is not of itself religious, and it will drop away as the husk drops from the ear of corn when ripe; and much more that is religious is not lost when it seems to be, but simply takes on another shape. Fruit-trees shed their sheets of blossoms, and for a space thereafter they make but very little show. Ignorant cavillers might sneer and say that their May wealth of promise and beauty was a short-lived thing. Exactly. But on those twigs whence the bloom has fallen is forming and maturing what is of far greater worth. And when the more manifest tokens of a religious awakening disappear.

and the tongue of unbelief talks merrily and flippantly. out the change, in many a soul there is quietly developing a devout, consecrated, active life. Anyhow, many an eye running over this page will look back through mists of glad tears to such times of grace and mercy, and many a heart will plead for their repetition. Indeed who is there that under these recitals of conquering love is not impelled to cry, "Send as Thou wilt, O Lord, only let Thy saints not slumber, nor sinners perish in their sins"? For us as Christian individuals and churches to go year after year, and see no lives regenerated, no hearts blessed with an unearthly peace, "is it not like standing among the gilded bottles of a dispensary, while death is desolating the town and your skill is inapt and your remedies impotent to save a single victim?"

We enter on no defence of modern revivals here. Less than this in passing, however, we could hardly say.

But by this time some one is ready to ask, what was meant by heading this chapter "Off on Furlough"? They reasonably and naturally ask, where the furlough for Uncle John has come in? Well, if by furlough is signified resting spell, he has not yet found it, nor did he ever find it till the last months of life were being spent. But these varied engagements and miscellaneous services came in after retiring from his first Tract Society labors, and before returning to its employ.

When his work in the Dutchess Association closed he had sixteen years yet to stay on earth. They were the most eventful and fruitful of his life. He goes to work now on a broader field. We will follow him there.

CHAPTER VI.

GOING TO THE FRONT.

"Lo, a cloud's about to vanish
From the day;
Lo, the right's about to conquer
Clear the way!
And a brazen wrong to crumble
Into clay."

THE dark days of 1861 came on. The nation was drifting into war. Few believed it, however, till the blow was absolutely struck. Then loyal millions arose and with one voice said, "Die who will or may, this land must live."

Everywhere were heard the shoutings of captains, the rattle of armor, the tramp of marching feet. Uncle John had been opposed to war. He had looked upon it as always a calamity, and frequently a crime. Again and again, regarding it through his strong affections and tender sympathies, he had shudderingly cried, "How long, O Lord, how long?" He had seen in the foe defeated and plundered a man and a brother. He had glimpsed the mutilations and barbarities and butcheries which war of necessity involved. He had heard the wails of orphanage and widowhood, and so recoiled from every appeal to arms.

But when the cup of trembling was put into his country's hands, and put into its hands unsought, he saw, as others did, that whatever its bitterness it must not be pushed away. For two years he listened, as did many heavy hearts, to tidings of drawn battles or defeats. Then he felt that his time had come, and that he had found his work. It was not to serve in the ranks: he was too old for that. It was not to act as an officer: for that he had no training and no taste. Another and a higher call was in his ears. There were sick and suffering men to be ministered to temporally and spiritually. That should be his task. He went to the Tract Society again, and asked if he could not have a new commission, a commission to engage in army labor. It was granted him in June, 1863, and he was soon inside the Federal lines,

> "Amid a wilderness of graves,
> With death on every hand."

Lee had started northward on that last invasion which he ever ventured, and whose issues half a dozen States a little later hung breathlessly on. Hooker's army was in full pursuit. The excitement was at white heat all over Maryland and along the Pennsylvania line. The cloud gathering so blackly was about to break. The rival hosts drew closer together, and finally grappled in one of the deadliest struggles of these latter days, on the ridges and slopes around Gettysburg.

It was the Sunday before the fight. The old Army of the Potomac lay stretched from Frederick City southward along the Monocacy. The "One Hundred and

Fiftieth New York," of which the writer was chaplain, had camped on a rough hillside. The regiment had as yet seen but little service; the march for days had been heavy; no one knew what moment orders might come to move on: so our meeting had been a short one and a small one that day. As it was closing, who should come in but Uncle John! These were all Dutchess County men, hundreds of whom he knew. Tired as they were, they were not too tired to welcome him. Moreover, he was recently from home, and to grasp his hand and listen to his voice seemed half as good as being there. Before daylight the advance was sounded, and all were tumbling out and falling into line. The columns went pushing along the artillery-rutted roads as if on a race toward those Pennsylvania hills. Uncle John was fifty years old or more, but he kept up with the best. Not only kept up, but often would shoulder for a mile or two the gun or knapsack of some poor fellow ready to give out. We missed him before getting to Gettysburg, and weeks passed before our men again saw his face. After the fight was over he became separated in some way from our troops, and was captured by Stuart's cavalry. "When brought into the presence of the general and questioned as a suspected spy, he instantly dissipated the suspicions of the officers by his frank and fearless words for the Master. 'I am working as a colporteur of the American Tract Society, to try and save the souls of the dear boys that fall around me daily. General, do you love Jesus?' The

General fenced the question with, 'I know that good old Society, and have no fear of its emissaries.' 'But, my dear general, do you love Jesus?' The puzzled officer was relieved by the suggestion of those who had arrested Uncle John, and who were already restive under his close questionings. 'General,' said they, 'take the man's promise that he will not tell of our whereabouts for twenty-four hours, and let us see him out of our lines, *or we will have a prayer-meeting from here to Richmond.*' And so it was decided. He made his way back into the Union lines, and was once more among friends."

He was only inside of the Confederate camp about ten hours, but it is doubtful whether in a like space so much Gospel was ever urged upon the men he met. And their supposition that he would have kept it up had he been held longer was perfectly correct. Had he been put in the foulest corner of Libby Prison, or Castle Thunder, the story of salvation would have rung there as it did in the jail at Philippi so long ago.

How he employed himself in the army one of the chaplains, Rev. E. J. Hamilton, tells us in a racy little sketch of the man which he prepared for publication while the war was yet going on. "Mark him as he enters camp. In his cheery way he says, 'How are you, dear boys? I am glad to see you. I guess I have a little something for you; I was thinking you would be wanting some paper or needles, for the paymaster has not been around in a good while, has he? I cannot carry much, but just step up, boys, and I will give you what I have.' Both his hands are busy dispensing sheets of paper, and pens, and thread, with skilful and impartial generosity. After these gifts tracts and religious reading are produced from the black satchel, and distributed to many glad recipients. Now his stock is exhausted, and after some excellent story or terse remark, he adds, "Now, boys, don't forget the prayer-meeting the chaplain is going to have this evening. Come, dear boys, and let us ask God to bless us.' 'We will, we will,' is the response of many voices, and possibly the evening hour will show that the invitation has been accepted by many silent, softened hearts that did not dare to speak. In the prayer-meeting he is a great power, for he generally imparts to his fellow-worshippers much of his own spirit. I first met him in the log church of our brigade. On that occasion he moved us all. After this I was going away for ten days, and asked him to look after my boys. He consented. On my return I was prepared for something of a revival, but not to learn that the chapel was crowded, and that meetings were kept up three times a day. When I entered it that afternoon what a scene presented itself! The place was half Babel, half Bochim. Many of the soldiers were kneeling, some praying, some sobbing, some groaning, some loudly responding. Uncle John was seemingly the most engaged of all. After the principal prayer was over he rose and in his sweet tenor voice began a favorite hymn. All joined, and the praise went up through the white trembling canvas roof. He had instituted the morning assembly for inquirers and young converts, that in the afternoon for the prayers and exhortations of Christians generally, while more formal exercises occupied the meeting at night.

"The evening service was the most important. Generally there was a sermon by one of the chaplains, after which those who loved the Lord and those who desired to do so were requested to remain. Commonly very few went away, and then Uncle John's work began. After some prayers and hymns he would make a short address, and conclude by asking those who felt themselves in need of salvation and who desired Christians to pray for them to stand up. And then what earnestness in persuading sinners to declare for Christ! He would look over the assembly sometimes for a minute till some one rose. 'There's one,' says Uncle John, with visible emotion. 'Bless the Lord. There is joy in heaven over one sinner that repenteth.' Then after a short pause he would add in the most inviting tones, 'And is there no other precious soul here that wants a Saviour? Yes, there's another. God bless you, dear brother. Oh, it was for such that Jesus died. Jesus, the Son of God,' and Uncle John would sing,

> 'He died for you,
> He died for me,
> He died to set poor sinners free;
> Oh, who's like Jesus
> That died on the tree?'

"Another pause. 'And is there not another one

who wants to love this blessed Saviour? Yes, I see you dear brother. I knew there would be more. I feel that God is here tonight. And there's another, and another, and another. Oh, praise the Lord! Precious Saviour, thy blood cleanses a universe from guilt.' In this way he would go on till perhaps a dozen or twenty had risen; then the meeting would be dismissed, and Uncle John and the chaplains would tarry with the anxious, conversing and praying according to the need of each individual case.

"During such an awakening Uncle John labors night and day. As he set out one morning to follow the impressions of the previous evening I went with him down the company streets. Entering a tent where two out of the four occupants were Christians, he addressed himself to each man and led in a short prayer. Then he asked for a sergeant whom he knew to be under deep conviction. The young man came in. Uncle John read the look of trouble on his face, and sadly and tenderly said, 'O Albert, Albert, my boy, haven't you given your heart to the Saviour yet? What is the matter? Why don't you throw every thing else away and trust only in the Lord Jesus? The young man answered that he was trying to do that, but could not find any peace. We all knelt down in the little shanty which barely held us, and the chaplain led in prayer. Then Uncle John said, 'Now, Albert, you pray.' The lad offered a few simple, earnest petitions, and we left him. Several days afterward I met him going to one of the meetings with a shining face. 'Well, Albert,' said I, 'how do you feel to-day?' 'Oh, bright as a shilling, chaplain,' was the singular but expressive reply. And bright ever since has been his Christian character and course.

"His fidelity is unsparing. 'Uncle John,' said one captain, 'I try to do my duty, and I think that is all that is required of me.' 'Why, captain,' answered the honest man, in tones of astonishment, 'how can you say so? No man does his duty who does not give his heart to God, and live in God's service. What would you think of a man brought up by a kind father, and provided by him with every means of happiness, who should be a good brother and husband and neighbor and citizen, and yet be a heartless and undutiful son? Don't you think his wickedness would be unspeakably great?' 'But the cases are different,' rejoined the captain. 'No, they are not,' said Uncle John. 'That man would be condemned by the moral sense of the community; and the godless sinner, you may depend upon it, will be condemned by the public opinion of the universe.'

"Nearly one hundred and fifty—one tenth of our whole brigade—professed faith in Christ during these services thus carried on. Many are in soldiers' graves, some are at home sick or wounded, some are in Southern prisons, but so far as I know the great majority have shown that their profession was well founded.

"On one occasion, I cannot say whether I was more amused to see the familiar yet respectful assurance, or gratified to witness the startling directness with which he interrogated a brave colonel whom he had never seen before. A meeting had been concluded in front of the headquarters tent, and Uncle John had conversed and prayed with a young man who had shown deep conviction and anxiety regarding his sins. Utterly unconscious of human presence, and with a simplicity and earnestness which rose above all influences of time and place, and surrounded themselves with their own proprieties—silence, solemnity, and attention—he knelt with the lad in the midst of a crowd of bystanders, and prayed for him, for his comrades, for the officers of the regiment, and for the whole army. The vigorous colloquial language of the prayer, and its particularizing petitions, in which names and places and circumstances were freely mentioned, interested and impressed the hearers of it. Conventionalities plainly had little to do with Uncle John's religion. The young man went away comforted, and trusting in God; and the crowd dispersed. Then we entered the colonel's tent, in which we found one or two officers of the command, together with their chief. After a few words of conversation regarding the history of the regiment and its part in the summer's campaign, in which it had lost heavily, Uncle John remarked that it was a blessed thing to have a hope that no bullet or cannon-ball can touch, and a life indestructible and immortal. Then turning to the colonel, he said, "And now, colonel, just tell Uncle John how it is with you. We are all perishing creatures, and must soon be in eternity together. Have you, dear colonel, a good hope in Christ? Can you say that you *know* that your Redeemer liveth? You will pardon Uncle John for asking you; he's a poor dying old man that loves your soul, and wants it to be saved." This appeal, made rapidly, without any apparent premeditation, and with great tact and tenderness, evidently affected the colonel. Uncle John proceeded in the same manner as before: "You know what I mean. I don't mean, Are you a professor of religion? for there are many unworthy professors; but, has your heart been renewed by grace divine? That is the point. Have you become a new creature in Christ Jesus? Have you experienced that change of which our Saviour speaks when he declares that a man must be born again before he can see the kingdom of God?" The colonel expressed a hope that he was a Christian; and Brother Vassar replied that he rejoiced to hear him say so; that he prayed the Lord to bless him and make him faithful to the end; and that he wished before God that all our leaders were earnest, believing men.

"During the revival in the winter he frequently moved the audiences in the log chapel with short but thrilling strains of extemporaneous eloquence. Those of us, who were accustomed to notice mental methods, could not but wonder at the man's gifts. For myself, I listened to passages in his oratory such as, I think, are seldom heard from either pulpit or rostrum. His style at times reminded one of the more serious and moving utterances of Gough. But his discourses showed more argument than is commonly attempted in those of that interesting lecturer. Thought after thought was presented and illustrated with admirable though untaught adherence to the rules of art. The logical order of the ideas, their progressive continuity of impulse, their practical development and application, were faultless. Homely condensed language, natural and striking metaphors, unexpected similes, antithesies and turns of expression, a becoming gesticulation, and a voice wonderfully persuasive and rich with sympathetic feeling, engaged attention, awoke the heart's best emotions and excited new interest and humble earnestness of the man was also a chief element of his power. Not a word was uttered for oratorical effect. Every sentence manifested yearning love for souls, vivid conceptions of eternal things, and a solemn sense of the presence of God. Success too, though confidently looked for, was expected solely through the divine blessing. What wonder was it that such speaking produced results that have been visible ever since? Those who have heard him will not forget with what joyous faith he sang,

> "Jesus shall reign where'er the sun
> Does his successive journeys run;"

nor how invitingly and solemnly he rendered

> "There is a fountain filled with blood,
> Drawn from Emmanuel's veins;"

nor the tenderness of those lines,

> "Come, trembling sinner, in whose breast
> A thousand thoughts revolve;
> Come with your guilt and fear oppressed,
> And make this last resolve;"

nor the heartiness of the verses,

> "Come ye sinners, poor and needy,
>   Weak and wounded, sick and sore;
> Jesus ready stands to save you,
>   Full of pity, love, and power."

How boldly he raised that Christian battle-song, "

> *"Am I a soldier of the cross?"*

What thankfulness and love he put into that grand hymn.

> "Oh for a thousand tongues to sing
> My dear Redeemer's praise!"

With what plaintive melody he sang,

> "Did Christ o'er sinners weep?
> And shall my tears be dry?"

and with what affectionate longing,

> "Jerusalem, my happy home."

These and many other old hymns, and the tunes which accompany them, were weapons of power with Uncle John.

During the early part of the summer he labored in the army of the James, among the colored regiments, and as might be conjectured, was very successful in arousing the lively African soldiers to the duties and attractions of religion. Nowhere were his visits more welcome, or the results of his efforts to lead men to the Saviour more apparent, than among the colored troops. They prepared a place in the pine woods with seats and a stand for speakers, where he often addressed them. From one thousand to fifteen hundred souls were frequently present at these meetings. It was a scene worthy of a painter's skill. I was particularly pleased with an address which he made one September evening in the plaza of

9

Fort Davis to a regiment drawn up before him in line. The colonel had directed a notification of the companies for a prayer-meeting which we proposed to have; but the adjutant, thinking, I presume, to do the business thoroughly, ordered out the whole command, as if for dress-parade. Uncle John stood with his hands behind him, leaning against a tree in front of the headquarters, while company after company filed past him, faced to the rear, and dressed into correct position. The men evidently were wondering what was going on; and some of the officers seemed to think that a joke was being perpetrated on the chaplains and Uncle John. However, we were ready for the emergency. A prayer-meeting was out of the question; so we resolved on some public exercises. After an introductory address, a hymn, and a prayer, Uncle John was invited to speak. He began by expressing his gratitude to the colonel for that opportunity of addressing the officers and men of "the dear old Seventh." He had come expecting only to attend a prayer-meeting, but was glad to meet so many brave men. As he looked on the faces before him, and saw how very few were present of those whom he had seen last winter, the thought arose, "Where were those brave boys that left the old camp at B.?" They are gone; they lie on the battlefields of the Wilderness, and of Spottsylvania, and of the North Anna, and of Coal Harbor—all along the way from the Rapidan to Petersburg. Some are at home in the North, or in hospitals; But how many occupy their long, last home—a soldier's grave! Scarcely one is left of the familiar faces. Ah, well did he remember some of those noble boys that he used to see in the old log chapel, and whom he should see never more on earth. But, blessed be God, he had a bright hope of meeting them in heaven. They were heroes of Christ, and of his cross. Now they have fought their fight, they have finished their course, and they have received their crown. Oh, how he wished that every soldier was a truly Christian man, and prepared for any chance that might befall him. He knew many brave men who were not Christians; but it was always a mystery to him how any man could face death without a hope in that blessed Saviour, who had triumphed over death and the grave. He supposed a sense of duty would do much, but how much better was it to be sure that one's soul has been saved with an eternal salvation. Then the king of terrors is dethroned, and death becomes the gate of heaven. Did you ever think, he asked, against what love you offend while you remain unreconciled to God? Oh, it filled all heaven with wonder, when God's glorious Son took on him our salvation, and offered himself for our sins. Never was love like His love. How can you refuse your hearts to that loving, dying Saviour? Surely you will not suffer it to be that Christ should have died for you in vain.

> "The Son of God in tears,
>   Angels with wonder see;
> Be thou astonished, O my soul,
>   He shed those tears for thee.
>
> "He wept that we might weep;
>   Each sin demands a tear.
> In heaven alone no sin is found,
>   And there's no weeping there."

Dear soldiers, if I know my own heart, I earnestly desire the welfare of you all. God knows that I love you, and want to see you happy. And when I think of the fatigues and exposures and dangers which soldiers must undergo, oh, how I wish to have them sustained and comforted by the hopes and consolations of the gospel. I would that every one of you had a sure title to a mansion in the skies. I would that you could all look from these scenes of conflict and suffering and death to that blessed land where there is war no more. Oh, yes; no whistling minie ball, no bursting Parrot shell shall disturb the peaceful inhabitants of that heavenly country. In that land there shall be rest for the weary; pain and grief shall not enter there:

"No groans shall mingle with the songs
That warble from immortal tongues."

Now let me say a few words to those of you who are Christians. Dear brethren, you are surrounded by temptations; but strive to live faithfully; hold fast your profession; let no man rob you of your crown. Trust not in yourselves, but in One who is mighty. Keep looking up to Jesus, and you will be conquerors, and more than conquerors, through him who loves you. Recently, by the bedside of a dear corporal that formerly belonged to your regiment, but who now sleeps in Jesus, I felt what truth, what power there is in the religion of Christ. All was peace with him, perfect peace. He knew that he was dying; but he rejoiced in the hope of a better life, in the sure prospect of a glorious immortality. "Oh, let me die the death of the righteous, and let my last end be like his." And as for you, dear friends, who are without Christ, will you not seek an interest in his salvation? Will you not begin to love and serve that Redeemer who can save and bless you for ever? Yes, Jesus is the Saviour that you need.

> "None but Jesus,
> None but Jesus
> Can do helpless sinners good."

Oh, then, do not hesitate. Tomorrow may be too late. Who knows how soon the bolt of death may come? Now, while it is called today, give your hearts to God, and kneel before him in penitence and prayer. Dear soldiers, I thank you for the kind attention with which you have listened to me. May the Lord bless you all, and bring you to his heavenly kingdom.

Such, as nearly as memory serves me, was the course of thought and style of language employed by Uncle John. But the sketch can give no adequate idea of the living power with which he spoke. His allusions to the uncertainty of life and the nearness of death had a peculiar significance with those whom he addressed. Several of their number had been instantaneously killed, not long before, on the picket line in front of the fort; and a day or two subsequently to our meeting, one poor lad was struck by a minie ball and died in five minutes, a few paces from the spot where he had listened to Uncle John. The summer's campaign had made us all too much accustomed to these things."

Rev. J. H. Twitchell, of the Asylum Hill Congregational Church, Hartford, Conn., who as chaplain was also thrown into such contact with him in the army, in

9*

a sermon to his people after the death of Uncle John recalls many interesting incidents. We can quote but a few.

"One evening a fellow-chaplain brought him to my tent. We had not met before. At once he burst out in such a strain of religious conversation as I had never heard. At first I was repelled. It seemed canting and extravagant. I could not believe it was genuine. But that suspicion did not last long. I soon saw that what he said, and his way of saying it, was the true utterance of the man. I cannot altogether describe the impression he made. I know that when he left I 'followed him out and yielded to the impulse that was strongly upon me to tell him I feared I knew but very little of what it was to be spiritually blessed, and to ask him to pray for me. His riches, convicted me of poverty. And I have heard a good many say that meeting him produced a like effect on them. There was a Unitarian chaplain amongst us who confessed that Mr. Vassar was a new exhibition of Christianity to him.

"In a merely physical point of view his achievement was prodigious. He began his day at roll-call, and was in a state of intense activity from sixteen to eighteen hours. He ate little, and slept little, yet never flagged, and never gave out. Week after week, and seven days in the week, the same even high rate of energy was sustained. I suppose there were very few of the eight thousand officers and men of our division with whom in the time he was with us he did not talk, and with the majority of them more than once or twice. I used to see him *running* in his eagerness to get about. Yet he was as far as possible from being in a flurry. His restlessness was wholly external. He always knew exactly what he was after. His objects were distinctly before him.

"Conversing with from seventy-five to a hundred different men a day, he came to the fiftieth or sixtieth just as fresh in his manner, just as much interested, just as tender, as at the first. He wasted no words. He went right to the heart of his errand at once, and his bearing was such that it was hardly possible to take offence. Indeed it was said, and I think truly, that in the entire division he never met with but one positive rebuff, and that in the case of an officer in liquor. And the reason was, he was entirely self-renounced, and showed it. He represented the yearning heart of Christ. It was almost magical the power he had over men. One of our chaplains, taking him to dine with him one day, found no member of his mess present beside himself but the colonel. Now this colonel was irreligious, immoral and low-bred, and the chaplain feared to have Mr. Vassar say any thing to him, and I think had advised him to that effect. For a little while the earnest man held his peace; then pausing from his eating, said, 'My dear colonel, this is the first-time I ever saw you, and perhaps we shall never meet again. I am sure you will not think it amiss if I ask you whether you have an interest in the great salvation?' The chaplain's heart leaped up into his mouth. He expected an explosion; but to his surprise the colonel answered the question as simply as it was asked, and with entire civility, and even thanked him for expressing such interest in his welfare. Dinner over, the colonel said, 'Sir, would you like to talk to the men?' Of course Uncle John said Yes, and the colonel absolutely spent half the afternoon in walking with him through the regiment, and introducing him to knots of soldiers here and there, with, 'Here's a gentleman who has something to say to you, and you had better listen to him, for I think he is a good man.' The chaplain followed them around in amazement, and could scarcely credit his senses. The colonel was not converted, but for the time he was subdued.

"And so he passed around among us for a whole season, uttering one voice continually—the voice of the invitations of divine love. It used to be said that he left the print of his knees in every company street of our division. If this was not literally true it was essentially so.

"Such a ministry could not fail to be fruitful. Upon hundreds, probably upon thousands, of men he made his mark for eternity. Dear old man! How he loved, and how he was loved for Christ's sake! There were joy and sorrow in all hearts when he parted from us. And when, as we were met together in our log chapel the evening after he bade us good-by, one of our soldiers—a Methodist—prayed in stentorian tones, '*O Lord, we thank Thee for sending dear Uncle John Vassar to us, and may God bless him wherever he goes,*' a chorus of amens responded, and I saw the tears falling on many a rugged cheek. It is my conviction that few more gracious spirits have been given to the church of Christ in any age than he. The last day alone will reveal how much good he did."

Professor G. D. B. Pepper, D.D., of Crozier Theological Seminary, sends these reminiscences of war days: "I met your uncle for the first time at Alexandria, Va., in the winter of 1863-64. I had gone there to serve the Christian commission as delegate for the term of six weeks, and to their headquarters Uncle John delighted as often as practicable to resort for Christian fellowship. We saw him, however, far less frequently than we desired, for he was incessantly and intensely active wherever soldiers could be found. At the 'Soldier's Rest,' the 'Teamster's Park,' the 'Ambulance Stand,' the 'Slave Pen,' 'Detached Regiments,' 'Garrisons of Neighboring Forts'—anywhere, everywhere, untiringly he went. Though laboring specially for the Tract Society, he worked as cordially with the delegates of the Commission as though he had been one of them. Indeed, so full was he of Christ that he became at once identified with every Christian spirit met by him, and identified with all and every Christian work. Firm in avowing and maintaining his distinctive denominational views when occasion required, neither these views nor their maintenance served as a wall or even bar of separation from any person or thing that was lovely and of good report. He was as intensely and completely catholic in heart and word and life, as he was intensely earnest in his convictions and their realizations.

"More than any other man whom I ever met, or ever expect to meet, Uncle John excelled in the power of free, ready, wise approach to, and entrance into, the hearts of men with personal religious messages. Herein he was no respecter of persons. Professor or non-professor, privates or officers, black or white, it mattered not to him. Enough that all were men, and his Master was the Master of all, and had sent him, John Vassar, as His servant and representative to all. Not only was he not a respecter of men, but just as little was he a respecter of times, places, or occasions, save to observe those proprieties which few better understood. But he held that all times, and all places, and all occasions were the Lord's, not less than all men, and it was never in his purpose or practice to yield God's claims to the claims of men or devils.

"Yet I never knew that he gave to any man offence by this forwardness. He had such self-revealing, overflowing, outgushing, all-conquering good-will and Christian love, such natural freedom, heartiness, and geniality, all elevated and glorified by his deep Christian experience, and also so much of childlike simplicity along with the wise tact and address perfected by years of incessant labor, that he would have been a strange man indeed who would not have opened all the doors of his heart to Uncle John, and told the dear old saint to make himself perfectly at home, and do and say just what he pleased.

"But while all recognized in him a true friend, no one could ever make him a mere 'hail fellow, well met.' His dealings were always in the clear view of a hastening eternity and its tremendous realities. Herein he was a pattern *to* all chaplains, but certainly not a pattern *after* all.

"I have a very vivid remembrance of one night's experience with him in a revival meeting which was held at the quarters of 'The Fourth Delaware,' but rather on my own account than on his. He had for several nights taken long walks out from the city to aid the chaplain, and had expressed the special desire for me to go with him some evening. I complied with the request at the first opportunity. The meeting tent was crowded. The opening hymn was rung out with mighty power—of lungs at least. Uncle John then introduced me to lead in prayer. I thought to lead, but soon found a multitude praying thunderously, each his own separate prayer. Of course I observed, not *enjoyed*, a short season of *private* devotion, whose end was as unnoticed by the crowd as had been its continuance. Uncle John was busy with inquirers amid this tempest of vociferous exercises. It was nothing to him what *form* expression took, if he could only find sinners seeking a Saviour, or any one needing advice or encouragement. Of course I was a spectator unable to adjust myself to the turmoil. At length in the midst of the meeting my dear old friend came round to me and said, 'Come, Brother Pepper, come up here in front; there's *a little lull* in the meeting now, and I want you to speak to the boys.' 'All right,' I said, and went with him. He shouted to them a kindly introduction of me, and asked them to listen to his friend whom he had brought along. But even then there was *only* 'a little lull' in the storm. I stood for half a minute looking at my *audience*—ah, not audience—awaiting silence, when a towering shouter just in front, with evident disgust at this trifling, this waste of holy time, at once burst into a yell of petition, adoration, or something else, and I in dishonor fled to a corner of the tent.

"In such a scene, or any other, that burning spirit wrought on doing the 'one thing' needful. Blessed is he. Blessed is his memory."

Among the Christian officers who greatly helped him, and whom he regarded as a brother in the Lord, was General McAllister, of whom he makes frequent mention in his correspondence and reports.

This testimony General McAllister now sends concerning him:

"He was a man for whom I had the highest esteem and the sincerest affection; so I gladly send this slight tribute to his worth.

"He was constantly going from regiment to regiment, from tent to tent, relieving both the temporal and spiritual wants of the soldiers. When he had been absent for a time and returned, there was great rejoicing among officers and men that Uncle John was back.

"Upon applying at headquarters for permission to hold meetings, the answer always was, 'Go ahead. We know you are all right.'

"In his frequent visits to my tent we had many pleasant conversations about the war and the religious condition of the army, and the intense patriot, as well as intense Christian, shone out in them all.

"It was his custom before leaving always to pray with us, and in his prayer each individual present was mentioned. One of my officers who was frequently with us said, 'I can stand up under any man's prayers but Uncle John Vassar's.'

"During the winter of 1863-64 there was a great revival, and especially in the Third Corps. Meetings were held nightly, and thousands were converted. Often, not knowing that Uncle John was present, I would be surprised to hear his voice from the rear of the chapel in exhortation. Perhaps that would be the sixth meeting that he had attended that evening."

His good friend, Colonel A. B. Smith, of Poughkeepsie, then Major of the 150th New York, furnishes this sketch:

"We were visited by Uncle John several times, and he was always welcome to a part of my tent. He was unremitting in ministering to the sick and disabled. I knew him once to carry a box as large as a good-sized trunk nearly three miles on his back, filled with delicacies for our sick and suffering men. He was ubiquitous in the army. Came often, and always left his mark for the Master on every one he met. He waited for no formalities. His first remark would be, 'I hope this loyal blue covers a heart loyal to the Lord Jesus. He is the best friend a soldier can have. Tell me, is he your friend? Come over to the prayer-meeting tonight.'

"On Sunday, the 9th day of August, 1863, we were at Kelly's Ford, and Uncle John came to us and said, 'Shall we not have a little prayer-meeting tonight about sundown between the 150th New York and 13th New Jersey regiments?' 'It was agreed upon. He was the only man in citizen's clothes in all the Twelfth Corps. All our chaplains were away sick or in hospitals, and a hundred or two gathered at the appointed time. We sat around or kneeled upon the ground, and Uncle John prayed as he only could pray. The meeting was going pleasantly on when a soldier from General Ruger's headquarters stepped into the circle, and touching Uncle John, said, 'The general wants you.' Not the least confused, he said, 'Boys, go right on; the general wants to see me,' and he marched at the side of the soldier a prisoner over to the headquarters of the brigade twenty rods or more away. He was there accosted with the rough inquiry, 'Who are you, and what are you here for? You are not the chaplain of either of those regiments. We shot a man as a spy who came into our camp as you have come today. By whose authority are you here?' 'Oh, I know the whole of the 150th Regiment,' said Uncle John. 'I am an agent of the American Tract Society, and have a pass through the whole army of the Potomac from

General Patrick and President Lincoln. And now, General, do you love the Lord Jesus Christ? We can have a little season of prayer right here.' 'No, no,' said General Ruger. 'Here, orderly, take this man back, and I will see Colonel Ketcham about him.' So Uncle John was back before the meeting ended, and it proved one of the best meetings I ever attended in the army.

"On the resignation of our chaplain, Rev. T. E. Vassar, his Uncle John was unanimously elected to fill the vacancy. Army regulations, however, required that a chaplain should be an ordained minister, which he was not. A strong letter from the officers of the regiment was sent to his church at Poughkeepsie, urging them to call a council for Uncle John's ordination, he having been licensed as a preacher some time before. He went home to take counsel touching the step, and found his church fully ready to proceed. Some outside parties, however—and some who ought to have been the last to whisper it—hinted to him that he was looking to the chaplaincy from sordid motives, the desire for paltry pelf. That settled the question. Of all men he was the last to deserve a thrust like that. If ever there lived an utterly unselfish soul it was he. But he would not put himself where his influence might be injured by such an imputation. Back he went to his old work at twenty-five dollars a month, instead of a chaplain's hundred and twenty-five, the same loving, busy, devoted soul that he was before. Our Twelfth Corps was then sent to the West and South-west to follow Sherman to the sea, and we never had Uncle John with us again. He sent us, however, occasional letters still, and among those who survive and remember those days his memory is sweet.

"I have known the man since 1851, and only to love and almost adore him as the most perfect exemplifier of Christ whom I ever knew. He was one of God's own noblemen. Disciplined, tried, purified, he shone like burnished gold. Often I heard unbelieving officers say that if they could have a religion such as his they would prize it above all price. What he suffered and endured in serving Christ and his fellow-men, and what the grand results, the eternal day must be left to tell."

Rev. E. Owen, of Wyoming County, N. Y., has something to give us concerning these same years. "My first acquaintance with him was at Alexandria, Va., during the war, where I was then engaged as Superintendent of the Freedmen's Bureau. It was the day after I received the intelligence that my son had been killed in the army. Feeling the need of a human sympathizer, after pouring out my grief to the Friend above, I went in the suburbs to look him up. His heart, like mine, was bleeding, for he had just heard of the loss of a dear Christian nephew, a staff officer of Banks', in Texas, who had recently been drowned.* Common grief cemented our hearts from that very hour.

---

* Lieutenant A. H. Vassar, of the Thirteenth Regiment, Corps d'Afrique, drowned on duty near Point Isabel, February 6th, 1864.

"After that, as he passed back and forth in his work, we were glad to have him drop in for a few minutes at our home, or spend occasionally a night. Those were precious hours. There would be intervals during which he would wake from sleep for a few minutes, and the first conscious breath would be prayer and praise. Soon as ever the day dawned we would hear him say, 'Come, brethren, let us be up and about the Master's work.' In connection with no life have I been so deeply impressed with the truth of that expression,

'Prayer is the Christian's vital breath.'

He seemed greatly to enjoy the social hour, but if conversation was leading off the track, he would cxclaim, 'Brethren, we must keep praying,' and forthwith drop down upon his knees, and draw all wandering thoughts back to God and duty at the mercy seat. One remarkable feature of his prayers, and which, apart from their special unction, made them so interesting, was the fact that he remembered the names and condition of those whom he had met, and formed them into petitions so forcible and appropriate as to give his supplications a freshness and variety seldom witnessed, and to fasten them as a nail in a sure place to produce effects likely to be lasting.

"After taking his long and weary tramps from regiment to regiment, literally loaded with books, tracts, papers, and other necessaries for the soldiers, he would sometimes return with his shoe-soles worn through to the very feet, but he scorned to rest while the neccessities of the times were so great."

10*

"His journeyings called into play his powers as a pedestrian, which were most extraordinary. He thought nothing of a stretch of eight or ten miles; and one hot summer day I knew him to walk fifteen miles and back again, with very little appearance of fatigue. It would be difficult, perhaps impossible, to find another man in the country as well qualified as he was for religious labor among soldiers, at least for that kind of labor which Uncle John performed. And certainly no one could enter upon such work with more self-devoting zeal than that which animated this singularly-gifted man.

"When I think of Uncle John as a ready and mighty laborer in the cause of man's regeneration, and compare him with what he was, the lively and driving manager of work in a brewery, I exclaim, 'How powerful is the grace of God; what changes it can effect; how marvellously it fashions the most unlikely materials into blessed instrumentalities of good!' Under its influence, abilities and habits developed in a life of eager worldliness are employed with singular efficiency in the pursuit of heavenly objects; the want of early preparation and instruction is compensated by the improvement of a devoted mind; and a holy consecration of purpose is unflinchingly sustained for years, and crowned with ever increasing success. Such an instance is rare; so that none should presume to squander precious time in the hope of future faithfulness; but what encouragement it contains for those, of whatever age or condition of life, who feel themselves called to some special department of the service of God."

But it is time we let the intrepid toiler tell us a little concerning his work, and tell it in his own words. There are letters and reports in his handwriting which would fill a volume such as this touching the labors of these days.

When in the autumn of 1863 the advance on the Rapidan was made, he says:

"We followed the poor boys out part of the way to the Rappahannock, and as they cried, 'Good-by, Uncle John,' the big tears rolled down many of their cheeks. We felt deeply for them, and soon the roar of cannon told us they had met the enemy in mortal combat. In the morning ambulances of wounded men came in calling for food and nursing. We joined the Christian Commission in its labor of love for two days, and passed through many affecting scenes."

A month later he is back at Alexandria in the "Soldiers' Rest," and thence he writes: "I have helped in two meetings a night for some time. The attendance is large, and many are serious, while a few have confessed Christ."

Here he meets the venerable Jeremiah H. Taylor, of Connecticut, a brother of James Brainerd Taylor, of saintly memory, a man who as this sentence is flowing from the pen is entering on his eighty-third year, but was then laboring for the bodies and souls of the soldiers with great diligence and success. These missionaries, thus brought together, were true yoke-fellows, and when the younger entered upon rest the elder toiler traced with trembling hand this testimony to his departed friend.

"It was my blessed privilege to be a fellow-laborer with this dear brother in the war. I never saw one on whose tongue the precious name of Jesus dwelt so much. It was the key-note to every utterance, it was the mainspring of all toil. How he unites now in that anthem of Paradise 'unto Him who loved us.' "

To which another adds: "No quiet for him even in heaven. He used to tell the people who were so fearful of excitement in religious services, that they would not be still after they left this world, for all heaven resounded with hallelujahs.

"Oh, what a great, gentle, strong, sweet soul he was. How near he kept that soul to God. Wherever he was, if the slightest shadow or sense of enfeeblement came over his spirit, he would stop short and gird up the loins of his mind by an appeal of childlike faith, an act of fresh surrender, or an outpouring of loving aspiration toward God. This infantile faith was what made him great before God, and this intense love made him mighty through God with men.

"It is the seen and claimed promises which make the clouds disperse and the heavens glow."

"There was no vital force lost in trimming his conduct to suit one eye fixed on the earth, and other eye looking toward heaven. The thought that he worked out in his life was, "Precious Jesus, draw me and I will run after Thee." It was Jesus in regeneration, Jesus for growth in grace, Jesus in life, and Jesus in death.

He was a burning and a shining light.

"As beacon lights, oh, may we stand,
Upon this dark and dreary strand;
To guide earth's voyagers through the gloom, To the
bright world beyond the tomb.
"Jesus, thou light from heaven divine,
Let thy bright beams within us shine;
That so our lives may ever be
A true reflection, Lord, of thee."

Hear the toiler again: "Last evening we heard from several converts in Battery H. It was worth all my labor here to listen to the story of what grace had done for them. At the Soldiers' Rest one fine young man cried out, ' O that God would have mercy on me. My mother died but a few days since, and begged me to meet her in heaven.' Another told me that he had left home to get rid of his mother's entreaties and prayers, but the Spirit had followed him and rung them in his ears. He has had a hard struggle, but I believe has submitted his heart to Christ."

Later in the winter he is down among the huts and tents of the Third Army Corps.

Rejoicingly he reports to the rooms in New York marvels of saving grace. "I have never seen such a work since coming out. There are crowded meetings every night. Christians are all aroused. Converts are being multipled. In the spring the entire command will move, and many of these will go out to die on the bloody field."

A chaplain at the same date writes to the Society: "We are greatly indebted to you for sending Uncle John here. We wish he could have remained all winter. When he bade us good-by it was with prayers and tears that reminded me of the elders parting with Paul at Miletus. He went away with his knees all ragged, like a scarred veteran."

He runs home for a few days, and on getting back to Washington finds that he cannot get at once inside our lines on account of some new orders which have just been given. No time must be lost, so he goes to work among the troops around the capital. We can imagine how he would enjoy a service such as this: "Sunday afternoon General Briggs, who has charge of all volunteers passing through here to the front, went with me to a meeting in a Pennsylvania regiment, where we had present a thousand officers and men. I wish you could have seen the General as he faced these men, and heard the words he pressed upon their hearts. I have not met such another Christian officer excepting General McAllister. Old Massachusetts may well be proud of such a son. He is a tower of strength to Christian laborers here.'

After the terrible battles in the "Wilderness" he went down to Fredericksburg, where the wounded had been brought in, and thence he writes: "I am surrounded by the dying and the dead. From morning to night, and often through the night, I am called to aid temporally or spiritually those who are nearing eternity. I have not passed by the poor rebel soldiers. Some of them were very grateful for kindnesses shown.

"I have been detailed with several others to nurse and care for some five hundred of our wounded men.

Many of them know me, and a number, when undergoing amputation, would beg me to come and stand by their sides. Thank God for our holy religion. In the midst of so much suffering I see some great triumphs of grace."

Next he is with General Butler's army at Point of Rocks, ministering to those in the convalescent camps injured in the attack on Petersburg, and this is the story that he tells: "I cannot describe what my eyes have seen, my ears heard, and my heart felt these ten days past; feeding men whose mouths have been torn by bullets, or whose throats so injured that they could hardly take nourishment sufficient to sustain life, distributing the stores of the Sanitary and Christian Commissions, praying with the dying, relieving men who for six weeks have been over the suffering or burying the dead—this has been my work."

From before Petersburg, where the Sanitary Commission finds in him a valued helper and puts large supplies at his disposal, he reports: "The firing is almost continuous along portions of our line. Many of the dear converts of last winter are falling, and are being laid to their long rest. One of them I had looked to as chosen of God for great good. Talented and generous, courageous, yet childlike, I have not often met his like. I saw him after he had fallen, the stars and stripes yet in his hands. His face was as radiant as when we last sang with him his favorite hymn, 'There is an hour of peaceful rest.'

"Another dear spirit was cut down in a recent

charge. I saw him after the amputation of his leg, and before he died. He seemed calm, cheerful, and full of delight in Christ. Speaking of his part in the engagement, he said, 'I did all I could.' These and many others are buried close up to the enemy's lines, but the loving Jesus watches over them as though they slept in the old family burial ground.

"One of the converts, after the explosion of the mine, came out badly hurt. He was placed among the wounded, and when I reached him he lifted up the stump of a missing limb and cried, 'Uncle John, I have lost my arm, but I have not lost my hold on Jesus.' "

"Nothing could be more conclusive as to the soundness of his work than such a testimony."

At City Point, amid the trenches, he was completely prostrated, and lay for days very ill. Ex-Mayor Fay, of Chelsea, Mass., took him to his tent and showed him such attention as a brother might. By Thanksgiving (1864) he is able to work again, and thus mentions the observance of that day: "We had religious services in all the forts and trenches, and at the hospitals and headquarters.

"Several more good boys belonging to our Christian brotherhood are gone. Sergeant L— was brought in dead while I was standing in the fort. A ball passed through his body. He never even groaned. When they picked him up Chaplain H— told him to look to Jesus. He looked up, and calmly said, 'Jesus is with me now. God's will be done.' "

On the first Sabbath in February, 1865, he writes

from Patrick's Station: "We had expected to dedicate several new log chapels and have some very interesting services today, but as we were getting ready the men were suddenly ordered to move to the left. For the last half hour the roar of cannon has been very hard. Some of the men who were so happy in our meeting last night, and who went out so cheerfully this morning, have been brought in dead. My heart sickens as I look on the bloody ground and remember what sorrow will be brought to many a home by this day's fight."

After the battle of Hatcher's Run comes this striking incident: "At one of the recent meetings this fact came out. In the last move a Christian young man in the camp was detailed to remain behind for some service while an impenitent tent-mate was ordered on. Anxious for the yet unsaved comrade, and fearing that the engagement might be a serious one, the pious soldier offered to change places with his chum, saying frankly that he believed he was prepared for whatever might come. The offer was accepted, and in the bloody battle that followed the friend who went was three times hit, but not seriously hurt. The impression made on the other soul was so deep as to send him at once to Christ."

Another, then a chaplain, Rev. L. R. Janes, now of Jefferson County, Tennessee, thus witnesses of Uncle John's services in the camp:

"I first met him in a field hospital at City Point, Virginia, and must confess that I did not immediately understand the man. I saw at once that he was a decided character, and very quickly discovered that he was all on fire with love to Jesus and his fellow-men.

"Learning of my position, he sought to secure my co-operation in a plan of work embracing the entire brigade. I entered into the arrangement, though with little of his faith. Wickedness was peculiarly rife, drinking, gambling, and the like prevailing all along the line. He knew that well, but he walked not by sight.

"Through the Christian Commission he secured for our use a chapel tent, nightly services were commenced, and for several weeks, until the army moved, a glorious and sweeping revival was enjoyed. Brother Vassar was very modest through it all. Although the prime mover, he invariably sought to bring the regular chaplains to the front, so that the most scrupulous sticklers for propriety could not have complained.

"Of course the worldly minded could not appreciate his consecration. Some of them insisted that the good man was partly crazed. My colonel was quite reluctant on this account to have him come before our regiment. It was not long, however, before he changed his mind. While lying in a hospital wounded, Brother Vassar called on him, and so won him over that, on returning to his command, he said, 'Uncle John's about right after all.'

"Upon my own mind he has ineffaceably stamped the impress of the thought, of which he was a living exemplification, "not with eye-service, as men-pleasers, but as the servants of Christ, doing the will of God from the heart.""

Chaplain H— says: "His pleading, particularizing prayers; his varied, choice, and ready store of hymns; his rapid, yet unoffending directness of personal appeal; his easy and quick command of thought and language; his homely, pointed, and solemn method in public address; and his very appearance, and voice, and manner, unpretending and deferential, yet as earnest and sympathetic as they possibly could be—all qualified him to succeed anywhere.

"I have been amazed sometimes at the beauty of his prayers. On one occasion, during the heat of summer, we rode together through the woods to a distant pasture, that our horses, then fed only on grain, might enjoy grazing for an hour. Uncle John had been somewhat depressed, and we sat under the shade of a tree. Suddenly he exclaimed, 'Brother H—, let us pray,' threw himself forward upon the grass, and instantly began, 'O God, on this beautiful day, amid these old woods, and beneath thine own clear heavens, we lift up our souls to Thee.' His voice, at first slow and full, was rich with melody and pathos; and as petition after petition, exquisitely expressed, followed each other in beautiful succession, I thought the sacred eloquence of that unstudied prayer such as I had never heard before. While the prostrate body rested on hands and knees, crouching in lowliest humility, and the face, with close-shut eyes and intensity of expression, sometimes almost touched the ground, the longing, believing spirit seemed to rise, as on angels' wings, into the presence and glory of its God. As we were returning, he said that he seemed to have had a glimpse of heaven, and was refreshed and comforted. I could easily believe it.

"I shall not soon forget the delight with which I first heard him singing a song, whose lively notes and cheerful, rejoicing confidence accorde admirably with his own spirit. It was towards the close of a crowded meeting in the log-chapel. He rose after a prayer, and turned round in the aisle so as to face the congregation. His right hand held the left by two fingers, and kept it out of the way behind his back. Standing in his humble, but easy manner, he began in a clear voice,

> " 'We are joyously voyaging over the main,
> Bound for the evergreen shore,
> Whose inhabitants never of sickness complain,
> And never see death any more.'

Warming as he went on, he kept looking over the audience to observe their feeling; and before he had finished he was clapping his hands quietly in time to the tune, and leading us all in the chorus, like an enthusiastic singing-teacher. The hymn, though familiar now, was then new to most of us, but we could not help joining with Uncle John, to the best of our ability, in the chorus. Few, perhaps none, went away from the meeting that night without resolving to secure transportation in that good ship, for which, according to his wont, Uncle John was looking up passengers."

Sunday morning, April 1st, 1865, was what might be properly called the last Sabbath of the war. Of that day, and those immediately following, let us hear what he has to say.

"Sunday morning dawned on a field of strife and

blood and death. Such a Sabbath I had not in all my army experience seen. For three miles I passed along the lines amid roaring cannon and bursting shells, where the 'gray' and the 'blue' often lay close together, mingling their life-blood and dying groans. We little realized in the confusion and horror of that day that the God of our fathers was using our men to strike the blows which should bring the long conflict to an end.

"Monday morning found our great army in pursuit of Lee and his troubled host. We followed with out sanitary wagons until we reached Burkesville. By that time so many had been wounded that the surgeons decided to establish a hospital there. In that I have busied myself for days. As we moved along the roads the colored people flocked out to see the 'Yankees,' as they called us, and in many queer ways they expressed their joy. One shouted, 'Ole Virginny neber tire, *but now she tire.*'

"Now we have the glorious news that General Lee has surrendered. Praise the Lord, O my soul. Many of our poor wounded boys have almost forgotten their sufferings in their joy over the report."

Immediately on the occupation of Richmond the Tract Society sent Rev. G. L. Shearer there to take charge of its work in Virginia, and for some months Uncle John was his efficient ally in trying to repair, morally and religiously at least, the ravages of war. To a later chapter these labors properly belong.

His army work was done. He had lived to see an

11*

honorable peace shed its light on the banner of stars. He had lived to see the monstrous evil, which had been his abhorrence always, and which had lain at the bottom of the struggle, not only shattered, but torn up root and branch. He saw guns stacked and swords sheathed, and battle-flags bullet-rent and powder-blackened hung up for a later generation's wondering eyes. He saw the white tents folded, the wards of suffering empty, and the lines of blue-coats melt noiselessly away. And nobody rejoiced more than he that the red river of blood had ceased to flow, that no more harvests would be trampled down, no more beds littered with the worn or maimed, no more households darkened and shivered, no more graves opened and filled. And yet with something like a pang, too, he saw the old regiments mustered out. A thousand memories, some bitter, some bright, linked him and the men with whom he had tramped and camped, and messed, and bunked, and suffered, and prayed, and praised. Long isolation from home had drawn their hearts together. From the fierce charge he had brought some back bleeding, and bound up their wounds. In the fever ward, where they had tossed and moaned, he had come to others and watched with the tenderness of a woman's love. With hundreds he had plead and wrestled when as penitent sinners they were looking and longing for the light, and rejoiced with them when as converts they saw the new and living way by which a contrite soul returns to God. With older believers there had been seasons of blessed communion; times when the fellowship of kindred minds had indeed been "like to that above." And beside the living there were the dead who had been left lying all along the line of march. Hours very sweet and precious he had spent with some of them. For a few he had even dug a grave, and wrapping their blankets around them, had lowered them into it, telling those helping meanwhile of that Christ Jesus who is the Redeemer and the Resurrection.

What wonder, if with devout gladness, and yet a trace of sadness, he saw this work end!

The results of these years it would be impossible to compute or calculate. We believe it perfectly safe to say that no single man ever performed in like space more personal labor, or amid like surroundings ever made a deeper or better mark on men.

For any thing more definite we must wait the disclosures of that all-judging day, whose reckonings will be correct.

CHAPTER VII.

NEW CAMPAIGNS.

"Where our Captain bids us go,
'Tis not ours to murmur No;
He that gives the sword and shield
Chooses too the battle field."

THE armies of the nation vanished as suddenly as they emerged, leaving but "the blessed memory of the rights they vindicated, and the honorable scars of the wrongs which they redressed." Chaplains who had been granted leave of absence from their flocks went back to lead them as aforetime through the green pastures and beside the still waters of Gospel peace. Uncle John did not follow the disbanding regiments northward. He saw a new field for operations opening in the States which war had stripped and torn and gashed. To enter it would require great tact and grace. Sectional animosities could hardly fail to be engendered during a four years' struggle, costing the lives of half a million men—animosities lasting and bitter and deep. This incident, given by Rev. G. S. Mott, D.D., of Flemington, N. J., would probably be a fair illustration of the temper of those times:

"Soon after hostilities ceased, Uncle John was sent by the Tract Society into a certain section of Virginia to ascertain what the public feeling was with reference to the Society and its work. Among those called upon was a prominent Presbyterian clergyman, whom he met on entering the yard, or at the gate. On making known his errand the minister replied, 'Do you know what is in my heart?' 'Of course not,' said Uncle John, 'but I hope it is good.' 'Not at all,' was the reply. 'My feeling is to kill you. I hope God gives me grace to prevent me from carrying that feeling out, but now you know just how I feel toward the North.'

"Before the interview ended the angry preacher was thoroughly melted down, but the wrathful and vindictive spirit with which he greeted a brother Christian was a sample of the disposition dominant in those days." To overcome it would require calmness, readiness, self-control, and in a sevenfold degree that charity which suffereth long and is kind.

Those who did not know the man whom we are tracing may think it almost incredible that he should have possessed these qualities. To them he has been represented as an excitable, impulsive, emotional enthusiast, rushing hither and thither all aflame; and they cannot understand how such a character could ever have been a peacemaker, how such a zealot could have poured oil on troubled waters, how one so positive and even turbulent could have dealt effectively with fractious tempers and stubborn wills. We may not pause here to harmonize these apparent incompatibilities. The two sides of an arch toward the base seem opposing columns, but up above they lock together, forming one perfect whole. Human nature often wraps up what looks like incongruities, but symmetry is the outcome still. Certain it is that John Vassar was the very incarnation of fervor; it is just as certain that under the sorest provocations he with perfect patience possessed his soul.

As was intimated in the last chapter, the Tract Society opened a depot for its publications in Richmond in May of 1865. Rev. Geo. L. Shearer, as District Secretary, was put in charge. Uncle John was to push out as opportunity might offer, organizing Sunday-schools, establishing meetings, and circulating religious reading matter to such an extent as the Society might be able to provide.

Secretary Shearer gives this idea of the demand:

"All the churches are exceedingly destitute of any thing like religious literature. Their denominational publishing houses were consumed in the late fire. Sabbath-schools shared their libraries with the soldiers, and the usual wear for four years leaves little stock on hand. Seventy thousand dollars' worth of publications could be judiciously distributed on this field, and the need of colporteur labor from house to house is great."

Dr. J. M. Stevenson, who had been instructed by the Committee of the Society to make an exploring tour of the South in the early summer, gives these impressions through the columns of the *Messenger*. "There are yet difficulties in the way of a cordial intercourse with the people, and many still refuse fraternal greetings, but the better minds and hearts are flowing together. There are more than a million of whites and blacks in Eastern Virginia living on plantations, and these, if reached at all by the Gospel, must be reached by colportage for some time to come. In many places they have no money. One man said to me, 'I have not had half a dollar for two months.' An able and honored professor in college has sold his furniture piecemeal to get bread. Many once wealthy are pensioners upon the Government. Three thousand colored children are in the freedmen's schools at Richmond, and perhaps four thousand in Sabbath-schools."

These glimpses of the condition of things will show us what was now to be Uncle John's work for a season, what was to be the character of his new campaigns.

His first communication opens thus: "Reached Richmond Saturday, and the next day went into Dr. Jeter's Sabbath-school, where the reception was warm and kind. Afternoon went among the colored people, and had a cordial welcome. Evening had a good meeting among the soldiers yet remaining here. The next Sabbath went down to Petersburg, and there heaven was brought nearer to me than for weeks before. The remembrance of the days when we lay in the trenches here, and of the prayers that went up from lips now still in death, stirred me up to magnify the Lord. I spoke to a large gathering of colored people, and many hearts seemed touched. Eight asked prayers, and I felt that a work of grace had begun with many more.

"In the First African Church, Richmond, we had

another precious and powerful meeting. More than thirty were greatly troubled, and some wept aloud. A great awakening, I believe, is near. Oh, for youthful strength and heavenly grace to labor for my dearest Lord."

The prediction was quickly verified. This First African Church, which had been for years the rendezvous or headquarters of the colored Baptists of the city, and had a membership of over three thousand, was visited by a most remarkable outpouring of saving grace. At its height the body of the house was mainly filled with inquiring souls, and frequently its nearly twenty-five hundred sittings were all occupied before the exercises of the hour began. While the interest prevailed Uncle John met the members for prayer at daybreak. Till noon he visited and prayed in their families. At twelve he went into the colored schools and spent an hour with those who were specially concerned. At four o'clock he met inquirers along with the pastor. At seven o'clock he addressed the crowds that assembled from night to night. Nearly five hundred were added to this single church.

From Richmond he pushed out into the country around, Danville, Lynchburg, and other large places engaging him for a few days each. In the midsummer of 1865 he was travelling southward in the State, and stopping at a station on the railroad, learned that in some coal mines near there were large companies of freedmen who had no school, and for whom no one seemed to care. Such a statement was enough to interest him in their behalf. He found a planter three miles away who agreed to superintend a Sabbath-school. A little further searching, and a building was obtained in which to meet. Notice was circulated as widely as possible, and the next Lord's Day a hundred came together to be taught. He scattered among these spellers and primers, and put up a card large enough for all to see, from which he gave them their first lesson. So eagerly did the people avail themselves of the help thus proffered that the school proved a marked success at once. Inspired by it, they even started a day-school, taught by one of their own race. Out of that soon came a church; out of the teacher came a pastor, and on a subsequent visit Uncle John found a hundred converts ready to confess Christ. Is it surprising that he wrote, "I feel thankful that I was ever permitted to visit this place. I wish the friend that gave fifteen dollars to purchase the books that started that school could see it now, and into what it has grown. Surely he would praise God as we did yesterday."

Hear him again report: "Last Sabbath I visited the country near Powhatan Court-House, and established a Sunday-school in the woods. A hundred of the young and old attended, some of whom came five miles. A number of planters were present, who admitted they had never seen persons more anxious to learn. A log-house for the school will at once be built. I can get up such schools every week if you can give the cards and books. We cannot ask the colored folks to

12

pay for them. They have all they can do to get bread. At Dover, where I established a school a few weeks ago, I stopped on my return. Some of the scholars ran to meet me, shouting, *'Uncle John, I have learned to read a heap since you were here.'* Better still, more than fifty have turned to Christ."

As a slight rest from these exhausting labors, Uncle John several times came North, and in the larger towns of the Eastern and Middle States sought to raise funds for the Society wherewith to prosecute its Southern work. This was never, however, the service which he preferred, and perhaps it would be but the simple truth to say that it was not the service in which he specially excelled. He *could* sell books, and he *could* collect money. He did both. But he was not a great salesman, nor a remarkable financier. He had royal gifts, but they were of quite another sort. Sometimes one of his warm-hearted statements of Southern destitution would move many and secure a large contribution. This incident of the kind seems authentic: "In Northern New York a country Sunday-school, after listening to his portrayal of the state of things in Virginia, and the demands of the hour, poured all their available funds into his handkerchief, class after class contributing till more than eighty dollars had been given."

With the closing days of 1866 he gets over the line into North Carolina, where black and white alike give him the kindest of welcomes. On Christmas day he thus reports: "I have just returned from the Moravian settlement at Salem. I made the journey of sixty miles on horseback, through more than fifty of which I did not see a single school-house. Bishop Bahnson and his brethren were very cordial. They are a grand missionary church. Their mark can be seen in all that region. Numbers are coming to Jesus. Hundreds within a few weeks have made their peace with God."

South Carolina, Tennessee, and Kentucky he reconnoitres to see what prospects offer for educational and evangelistic work. He reports prejudices softening everywhere, but sore poverty amounting often to absolute distress. In the latter State he makes the acquaintance of an earnest Christian woman, concerning whom he tells this story: In 1863 one of Morgan's raiders was thrown from his horse near Lexington and mortally injured. He was taken to the house of this lady, who, while doing all she could to relieve his bodily suffering, labored assiduously for the salvation of his soul. After several days of keen distress Christ was revealed, and peace came. Before he died his kind hostess promised that his body should be taken for burial to his Georgia home. At the close of the war she fulfilled her pledge, and laid him in a grave by his father's side. While on this errand she was touched by the extreme destitution prevailing in that portion of the State. Many were going literally hungry, and of the means of grace there was an utter lack. She sent back to her own neighborhood an appeal for food, and vast quantities of corn were gathered up and forwarded to her for the relief of their more pressing wants. While superintending the distribution of these supplies she organized among whites and blacks *nineteen* Sunday-schools, and secured books and papers for their use. She now proposes to go into the mountain regions of her own State, where it is said that there are twelve thousand families without the Word of God, and make a similar effort. Who will help this self-sacrificing, heroic woman?"

What large results may be realized from small beginnings another letter of his, written about this time, tells. "In a neighborhood of Stafford County, Virginia, where there was no Sabbath-school when I first visited it, and where I could at that time get no one to engage in the enterprise, a lady tells me how God led her husband into the work. When he went home from our meeting he told her that he had lived fifty years without Jesus, but could do so no longer. He sent for a minister to come to his house and preach. The truth was blessed to his own salvation. Fifty others soon followed in his steps. A church was organized. A meeting-house holding two hundred has been built, and I remained and organized a Sunday-school in it, which will have a hundred children enrolled before the summer ends."

And a little later:

"By the help of God, I would plead for the poor white and colored people of this desolated part of our country, until every Christian and friend of his country shall feel the responsibility God has rolled upon us to help them in this hour of need. What shall be the character of this population? How may we labor to stamp the image of Christ on the hearts of thousands? These are weighty questions with me.

"I am busy every day and night among the colored people. Quite a number of our scholars in our Sunday-school have found Christ, and it is blessed to see their happy faces on Sunday morning as they make their way in haste to school. A large number are under conviction and need constant instruction. Hundreds know me, and cry, 'Uncle John, how do you do?' I am getting more and more interested in the children. I have thousands of nephews and nieces, and feel no shame as they recognize me as 'Uncle John.' All I want is to meet these thousands in the house of many mansions. Jesus will have many jewels set in dark caskets to stud his crown.

"A little beyond Oregon Hill, I passed over a large field of graves, where lay so many of the men of both armies. I thought of the many hopes buried with the bodies of the poor boys sleeping away from friends and home. My heart was touched with the remembrance of the past; but another feeling filled my bosom as I saw crowds of living forms, small and great, passing before me as I entered the city, and I looked upon the thousands I have been mingling with, I felt impelled to lift my heart to heaven for their salvation. Oh, that the church of Christ were awake to the interests of these unnumbered souls that are ready to perish in the midst of poverty.

"Such a field as we find in Virginia is seldom looked

12*

upon by Christian men. There are thousands of colored people who need to be taught to read and to be led to look to Jesus for salvation. In their unsettled state they need God-fearing men to encourage them religiously, and teach them in temporal matters what is for their good. Thousands of the colored people thank us for our labors and our prayers, and the poorer class of whites receive us gladly when they know our object in coming among them. Could we only have the books and men to reach the different counties of this great state, God only knows the good that might be done."

His labors here, and in his frequent visits to other parts of his field, were very arduous; but his heart was greatly cheered by the anxiety of the people to learn, and by the constant evidences of the Holy Spirit. "Two things," he says, "keep me from fainting by the way: the children learn so fast, and many are coming to Christ. Sometimes as many as fifty have united with the colored churches on a Sunday. They organize churches in the woods, and build log-houses to worship God in, and teach their children to read. Every visit to the country convinces me that we have the grandest mission field in America. In the widespread influences of the religion of Christ, I see the only great and permanent prosperity of the South."

Toward the autumn of 1868 he starts for Florida, and, while stopping at Savannah, he goes out to Bethesda, where under the grand old oaks Whitefield so often preached, and where he established his Orphan's Home. We can easily imagine how his heart could be thrilled on such ground, and what prayers there burst from his lips.

In Florida his good friend Dr. Bronson, of St. Augustine, formerly of New York, gives him a warm support. Uncle John here finds experiences rather rougher in some respects than any encountered heretofore. Let him describe some of the difficulties met. "I have concluded that I was led here to learn the apostolic mode of evangelization. I cannot say with the apostle that 'a day and a night I have been in the deep,' but I can say that I have waded through the water for miles, and often knee-deep, to reach the scattered settlements.

"Last week, with James Middleton, an old pioneer Methodist preacher, as guide, I attempted to reach St. John's County to establish a few schools. Sometimes for two miles at a stretch we went through water in the swamps and on the savannas from six inches to two feet deep. We kept up our courage, however, by singing,

'No foot of land do I possess,
No cottage in the wilderness.'

We made ten miles in five hours, and reached the end of our journey well soaked. *How delightful is this work for Jesus!* As I lay out all night last week I felt like praising Him aloud. Who would not gladly spare a few years out of heaven's bliss to gather jewels for the precious Saviour's crown? 'If we suffer we shall also reign with Him.' Oh, that we all might know the meaning of these words."

Stopping for a few hours with Dr. Bronson in his pleasant Southern home in the spring of 1870, we heard his testimony to the wonderful labors performed by Uncle John all up and down the St. John's, the heartiness with which the humbler classes welcomed him, and the blessings which everywhere crowned his toil. And at Green Cove Springs and Magnolia and Pilatka and Jacksonville black and white alike remembered him, and warmed up at the mention of his name.

In 1868 he spent some time in Central and Western New York, of which we get glimpses such as these:

"There was a revival in the Brick Presbyterian Church of Rochester, and Uncle John, accompanied by one of the elders, went from house to house.

"The elder felt quite nervous at the first for fear that something might be said or done which would be out of place or in bad taste. He was afraid that Uncle John, who was a plain man and fresh from army and freedmen's work, might be out of his element in mixing with a higher social class. But after the first two or three calls every fear of this sort was dissipated. He found Uncle John was equal to any place or class. He made no blunders, and was above and beyond criticism. To him it was a wonder that this man, untutored in social etiquette or conventionalities, struck so nearly right every time. Two or three things accounted for it. He had naturally the instincts of a true gentleman. He was quick to read human nature, and he had a large amount of sanctified common-sense which never forsook him.

"I once saw him ask a man if he loved Jesus. The man was a German, and could not understand a word said. Uncle John was not to be baffled by such a fact as this. He pointed with his finger upward, and with an expression on his face that spoke more than words, he caused his German friend to comprehend his meaning.

"One day while in Rochester he happened to be in the store of one of our leading business men, and, as was his wont, took the opportunity to speak a word on the subject of religion with those who came in. Some were evidently surprised, but none seemed offended. After Uncle John went out, a railroad conductor came in, who was rough and sometimes violent, especially if his prejudices happened to be crossed. What had been going on in the store was causally mentioned, whereupon this conductor exclaimed, 'Well, neither he nor any other man would dare try that on me. If he did he would get a piece of my mind.

"The very next day the two men chanced to meet there. Uncle John, all ignorant of what had been said, edged around to the conductor, and presently out came the inevitable question, 'My friend, may I ask if you love Jesus?' The proprietor of the store now expected a scene. Instead of that the man only stammered out a few words of explanation or apology over the fact that he did not. When Uncle John left, the conductor asked, 'Who was that man?' The storekeeper replied, 'Uncle John Vassar, the man I told you of yesterday.' 'Is it, indeed?' 'he said. 'Well, he is a good fellow any way.'"

Now he goes to minister to still another class. In the summer of 1869 the Tract Society determined to put its system of colportage in operation along the Pacific Railroad, among the mining regions of the Rocky Mountains, and up and down the country's sunset slopes. Mr. Shearer, so long in charge of the Richmond agency, was intrusted with the work, and to his assistance he called the man who had shared with him other trusts and toils.

In the cabins of Colorado miners we next find Uncle John. It's hard material that he here comes in contact with and seeks to mould for holiness and heaven. He takes in the situation at a glance, and says, "No man of weak faith and little love can succeed here. It will take a soul of the John Knox stamp to get hold of the men who venture here for silver and gold." But undaunted by what is unpromising, he strikes right in. Before he leaves, these adventurers and fortune-seekers are melted under the truth of God, as voiced by loving lips and energized by the Spirit's might. Hear him tell again the old story: "We had four meetings on Sunday, and I have not seen more tears shed for a long time. Strong men broke down as they were plead with, or while prayer was being offered in their behalf. A few very devout souls are to be found here, and I have enjoyed a rich feast of love with them."

He finds a little English lad in the boarding house who has recently given his heart to Christ, and he sets him to work distributing religious reading, and begs the brethren at the rooms on Nassau Street to send the young disciple longing to be useful twenty copies of the *Messenger* monthly to circulate.

At Virginia City, Sacramento, and at Stockton he labors for a few days with different pastors, and Mr. Shearer reports that this wayside sowing everywhere bears fruit.

In the first-named town on Sunday afternoon he exhorted in front of a noted gambling saloon. "The attendance was large and the attention good. Some at the close returned to their games disappointed that with such a crowd there could not have been so much as a dog fight; others wondered where the margin for profit could be, inasmuch as both the talking and the tracts were free; but in many ears the familiar, yet long-forgotten, words of entreaty, invitation, and warning came with an almost melting power."

In San Francisco an agency of the Society is established, and some stirring meetings held there, as well as at Oakland and other towns in the interior, or up and down the coast. The Chinese, that now vexing factor in the national problem, were then beginning to crowd over to our Pacific slope, and they greatly interested Uncle John. With one or two who had recently been converted he had protracted and pleasant interviews, for every redeemed soul his heart went out to as a brother's, whatever the nationality or name.

An influential pastor of the city, in communicating with the "Rooms," says: "The people are greatly in love with Uncle John, and I do not wonder. Wherever he goes the Lord is sure to be with him. He is now among Dr. Scudder's people, and the elders are going from house to house with him with tears."

While in San Francisco friends plan for him a little trip for rest. They arrange that he shall visit the Yosemite Valley, and see God's wonders in nature there. Always thinking of toil, and not of sight-seeing or ease, he doubts at first whether it will be right for him to go; whether it will not be misappropriating time—time which should be given to saving souls. His scruples finally are overcome, and with congenial companions he spends a week surrounded by what is stupendous and sublime. Mere recreation, however, by no means engrosses his time or thought. All the grandeur and beauty that meet his eyes are a mirror glassing the perfections of their Author, and his Father and Friend. All the while he is breaking forth in praise. When the Sabbath comes he and his brethren worship with a group of Digger Indians gathered around and looking curiously on. Oh, how Uncle John yearns for the ability to tell these degraded specimens of human kind of Jesus and His love! If he could have seen one of these stupid imbruted savages accepting Christ it would have delighted him more than the glories of towering cliffs and plunging cataracts. All he could do toward reaching them, however, was to pray God to speak to them by a tongue that they could understand.

On this Western trip he makes a brief halt at Salt Lake City, of which we have no record, but another Christian laborer subsequently appointed to that hard field found traces of his fidelity, evidences that he vigorously tilled a bit of that stubborn soil, and that the effort was not altogether vain.

Florida now claims him again for the winter. And the next summer Kansas is stirred by him as he pushes from city to city, and from town to town, seeking to interest Christian women especially and get them to organize local societies for the visitation of families and the distribution of tracts and books. A regular system is in many places introduced. The larger centres of population are districted, and delegates found for each section or street. Stated meetings are arranged for, with reports.

These in brief were the engagements and undertakings of what we have called his new campaigns. The freedmen, the poor whites of the South, the miners of Nevada and Colorado and California, the Mormons of Utah, the new settlers on the plains of Kansas and along her streams, the hardy mountaineers of Kentucky and East Tennessee—all were plied with whatsoever Gospel truth could awe or win, attract or alarm, and upborne on the strong arms of wrestling prayer.

The variety of incident entering into years of such service eventually becomes—thin and dreamy. It fades out of sight as the shore does to the receding voyager. Standing on the vessel's deck as it leaves port, the passenger sees object after object disappear, till finally even high-topped hills and the light-house on the rock are no longer visible. Time and its experiences so sink away. Occurrences which impressed us deeply at the first cease to be remembered as we travel on and they are left further off. If a tithe of what Uncle John has told us about the days just reviewed could be recalled and repeated here it would be of thrilling interest. Much of it would make the eye moisten and the heart glow. If forgotten by us, however, all these details and circumstances God remembers, and keeps them working in the wide scheme of an unsleeping providence toward the foreseen and foretold dominion of His Son. How vast may be the range of a blessing dropping first in a negro hut or a prairie cabin! Who can calculate the final issues of an influence for good starting on its line of march with a tract left at a door, or a prayer offered within? Who can limit the effect of an interview like this which we have heard Uncle John describe? We think it happened during his earlier labors in the West.

In one house that was entered the praying wife of an infidel husband begged that a Bible might be given her, as there had been none in the home during all their married life. One was furnished her, and the missionary went his way. Hardly had he gone out of sight when the husband came in, and instantly his eye lit upon the book. One glance aroused all his rage. Seizing the volume with one hand, and his axe with the other, he hurried out to the wood-pile, and laying it on the chopping-block, he cut it through and through. Coming back to the cabin with the two pieces, he hurled one toward the wife, saying in a mocking tone, "As you claim a part of all the property around here, there is your share of this." The other half was pitched up into a niche where tools were sometimes kept. Months passed. The timid wife could only pray. One wet or wintry day, when the man was indoors, with little to do, finding the time hang heavy, he looked around for something to read. Reading matter in that home was scarce. While rummaging around in this nook in search of some old newspaper, what should turn up but his half of the mutilated book. To while away the monotony of the hour he took it up. Was it by accident that he opened at the parable of the prodigal? He did not remember having seen it before. By its simplicity he was charmed. Presently the narrative was broken off. To finish it he must have the missing piece. Unwilling to ask for it, and so acknowledge that even his curiosity was stirred, he cast stealthy glances here and there to see if it would not appear. But its wary owner had safely hidden her fragment of Scripture, and his hunt was vain. Pretty soon inquisitiveness conquered pride, and at his request the wife produced her piece. The story was finished. It was read over again and again. Need the outcome of the whole be told? Another wanderer fell at the Father's feet. Another penitent was folded in the Father's arms. Another bitter opposer became the champion of a faith which all his life he had labored to destroy.

Had Uncle John emptied out that day on the cabin-floor bags of gold, that had been a smaller gift. Money might have wrought the godless settler's ruin. It might have helped perpetuate unbelief in his own and other souls. It might have blotted his name out of every promise and put it into every curse of heaven. The Book of God put into that home, with its blood of redemption, sealed his title to a celestial inheritance, and made the man the pioneer of other scoffers back to God.

Again we ask where the influence of one such occurrence is to end. Surely "the shock of the archangel's trumpet will not break it, nor the gulf of eternity swallow it up."

A friend sends the following narrative as related to him by Uncle John, which illustrates his habit as well as his success in following up a case.

"It was a great thing—one of the richest treats, to hear him relate the history of cases out of the journal of his experiences. No tale of adventure was ever more fascinating than these accounts as he gave them. I have known a tent-full of army officers, most of them ungodly men, listen to him a whole evening with the most absorbed attention while he described conversions that took place going on twenty years before. It is hardly necessary to say that under such circumstances his storytelling was always preaching in disguise. His style was all his own; he was an exceedingly rapid talker, full of life and action, and it would be impossible to reproduce his narrations of this sort. But one that I remember ran somewhat thus:

"There was a man in ———— county, a Mr. R——
who lived away from everybody in a log-house; I never
shall forget the time I had with him. Oh, how he *did*
hate to repent! But he had to at last. Grace was too
much for him. And then he had an excellent Christian
wife, as so many men have. That helped a good deal.
He was fond of his wife, and sometimes he overheard
her praying. He knew how she felt about it. I suppose
I saw that man twenty times. Sometimes he was good-
natured and sometimes he was not. How mad he would
be once in a while, just because I said a friendly word
to him about his soul! You see, he was not at ease in
his sins. Men never are. They try to be and pretend to
be, but they are not. They cannot be. The impenitent
sinner is not happy. This man used to be very angry
sometimes. But he never struck me. He came pretty
near it once or twice, and I thought he was going to,
but he did not. It was after I had known him a good
while, that one day when I had gone out into the lot
where he was at work to find him, he dropped his hoe
and came at me fierce as a lion, cursing and swearing;
I stood still and he stopped, and we stood and looked at
each other. Finally I said, 'O Mr. R—— , you will never
have any peace till you give your heart to God!' and I
know that I spoke kindly, for I felt just like crying, I
was so sorry for him. But it seemed to make him only
angrier still. He fairly foamed at the mouth, and, shouting at the top of his voice, he told me to leave and never
let him see my face again, or he would kill me. I did not
answer a word, and walked quietly away; but I felt pret-

13*

ty sure that the end was near, and that he could not hold out much longer. The next time I came that way, as I approached his house, I thought I saw him slip around the corner of the house and make for the barn, like a person trying to get out of sight. I went to the door and asked his wife where he was. 'Oh, my poor husband!' she said, and the tears came into her eyes. 'Have courage,' I said; 'I believe the Lord will find him this day. Where is he?' He told me not to tell you where he was,' she replied. 'He saw you coming and went out to get away from you, but—but—I think he went toward the barn.'

"Now, dear sister,' said I, 'you stay here and pray, and I will go and try to find him.' I went out to the barn. I knew that his proud heart must be giving way, else he would not have avoided me so. I tried one of the barn doors. It was fastened. I knocked. No answer. It was as still as the grave inside. 'O Mr. R——,' I cried, 'let me in, *do* let me in! I'm nobody but a poor sinner saved by grace, and the same grace will save you, if you will only let it! Let me in for Christ's sake; please do!' Then I passed around to another door and found that fastened, too, and knocked there, and again I begged him to let me in.

"At last, when I began to be afraid I must give him up for that time, as I listened, I heard a sigh and a step; then more steps coming toward me. I heard him unlocking the door. I did not know what was going to happen next. The door opened slowly, and there he stood. You needed to look but once to see that the

Lord had won the fight. His face was pale, but there was no anger in it. He tried to speak but he could not. I went right up to him and took him by the hand, and said, 'O my dear Mr. R—, let us kneel down and thank God together' and so we did. There were a good many more tears in that prayer than words. 'Now,' said he, as soon as he could control his voice, 'let us go in and see my wife.' I tell you the two minutes it took us to go from the barn to the house were the happiest two minutes he had ever seen. And you ought to have seen that woman's face when she saw us coming in together! She knew what it meant. Besides, a single glance at him was enough. It seems to me I never saw so happy a woman in my life.

"Uncle John accepted fully Rutherford's exhortation: "Take as many with you to heaven as you are able to draw; the more you draw with you, you shall be the welcomer yourself."

We are brought now down to 1871. Uncle John has seven years remaining in which to war the good warfare. It will be carried on in what might be called "the Department of the East."

CHAPTER VIII.

ALL ALONG THE LINES.

"Every battle I shall win,
Triumph over every sin,
'What!' you say, 'a victor be?'
No, not I, but Christ in me."

IF there is any one part of our country which more than another might seem to have little use for such a man as Uncle John it is the New England States. Settled by men characterized to a pre-eminent degree by regard for religious things, populated still chiefly by their descendants, studded with churches whose pulpits are occupied by preachers inferior in ability and devotedness to no others in the land, blessed with revivals reaching wide and deep, it would look as though these ancient Christian commonwealths would have little work for a colporteur anywhere within their bounds.

It is a fact, however, that old-established churches, and communities long leavened by gospel truth, sometimes need to have their decorous and conventional ways broken in upon as the smooth religious life of eighteen hundred years ago was broken in upon by "the voice of one crying in the wilderness."

There is such a tendency to get into ruts of creed and conduct, and go jogging monotonously along them, that every now and then something needs to occur that shall start us out of them, and make religion seem an awfully earnest thing. Hence it was that Uncle John was invited to labor in strong churches of Massachusetts and Connecticut, the history of some of which runs almost back to the coming of the Mayflower, as well as amid their rural neighborhoods in which, on account of removals westward or the concentration of population in the manufacturing towns, gospel influence had to some extent declined. In these States he spent a large part of his last half dozen years; but as Maine, Rhode Island, New York, and New Jersey shared his labors during that period to some extent, we attach to these scattered operations the caption, ALL ALONG THE LINES.

Christian brethren in the various communities thus visited send accounts more or less complete of the way God wrought through him and by him to arouse and save.

Rev. I. C. Meserve, of New Haven, Conn.: "I had just entered upon my ministry when I first saw him. He came to my study to see me, and at first I thought him some harmless but decidedly crazy man. In less than an hour, however, the truth broke in upon me that a Christian was in my house of a type hitherto unknown. He stayed a few days with me and we then formed a friendship which death has not severed and which I count one of the richest treasures of my life.

"Two or three incidents occurred that most admir-

ably illustrate his spirit and his methods. This as showing the temper with which he met rebuff. One day we
met a prominent church member. I introduced them,
and the conversation was not long in reaching the
plainly but kindly put question, 'Are you a child of God,
and how is it with you?' The angry and unexpected answer was, 'I don't answer any such questions. I don't
do business that way, sir.' Uncle John took no offence,
but simply explained that as a member of the Lord's
kingdom he wished to communicate in the language of
that kingdom with any fellow-member whom he met.

"We passed on and soon saw a man approaching who
was not a believer in a personal devil. I so informed
Uncle John, who, on being introduced, went on to state
that he was a colporteur of the American Tract Society,
travelling over the country fighting the devil; 'And do
you know, brother, I find some people who don't believe there is any devil; but you and I know that these
are his greatest dupes.' It was a master stroke of policy
and tact and skill.

I saw him with an old man of more than eighty who
had resisted gospel influences all his life, and apparently was totally unconcerned. In ten minutes his indifference melted, and with flowing tears he confessed his
need of Christ. I watched that encounter with intense
interest, for it was like a duel of wit and argument, and
discerned that the rarest powers in soul-searching
were possessed by Uncle John.

"For three successive winters he helped me when I

was pastor of the little church in State street, Brooklyn, N. Y., and under God I believe he saved it from disbanding in despair. Such praying and pleading in public and private—my heart grows hot with the memory of it.

"I saw him on his knees one day in our lecture-room at the close of Sunday-school, pleading for the children, some of whom were gathered around. I watched to note the effect of the prayer. Presently a boy a dozen or more years old dropped on his knees, then he crawled under Uncle John's uplifted arm, and finally threw himself sobbing upon that broad breast, as true a Christian from that hour forward as I ever met. Others followed, and the dear old man was presently surrounded by a group who were led to the very foot of the cross by that prayer. And it was not undue excitement either. I want to bear witness to the fact that those who were converted under his labors were as reliable in their after lives as any Christians whom I have known. The lad spoken of became a power in the church, and in his own home too.

"And I want to speak here of a prayer-meeting in my own house one night, in which I came nearer realizing heaven upon earth than ever before or since. We had been having a blessed time at the church that night, and from it came back—my wife, my brother (then preparing for the ministry), and myself. After a few minutes' conversation Uncle John suggested a season of prayer together before going to the night's rest. The memory of those next minutes will only fade with life. With melted hearts and streaming eyes by way of Calvary we drew near our Lord. Uncle John seemed to me that night like a guide who knew every inch of the road and took us right into the secret place of the Most High.

"After I came to New Haven to take charge of the Davenport Church, he labored with me between two and three weeks. The number of converts was large, but the impetus given to the spiritual life of the church, and especially the type which its character took on was so marked that its progress has been wonderful. Hundreds have been attracted to it, and I am confident that it was largely because of Uncle John that these blessed results came.

"Of one more fact let me tell. He went by invitation several winters ago to one of our Connecticut towns, and was met by a spirit of decided opposition. Some threatened to personally maltreat him if he ventured into their homes. So wonderfully, however, did God work that in a few days he was in those very houses, and greeted with a 'Come in, Uncle John, we have been waiting and wanting to see you here.' The witnesses of his power over the minds and consciences and hearts of men are numbered by thousands in New England, and all because he was, as much as any prophet of old, 'a man of God.' "

Rev. Mr. Zabriskie, now of Wollaston, Mass., furnishes the following graphic sketch:

"One afternoon, in the summer of 1872, I received a call at my parsonage at Old Saybrook, Conn. I did not catch the name of my visitor so as to recognize it, and on entering the reception room I looked with some suspicion on the travel-stained man whom I found waiting there. I received so many itinerants of various degrees of dubiousness, that I had come to throw the burden of proof on them in the establishment of their genuineness and respectability. But by and by as it dawned on me that this was Uncle John Vassar, the modern successor, if not of the apostles, yet of the 'seventy,' and the latchets of whose dusty shoes I was not worthy to stoop down and unloose, there was a sudden and decided revolution in my mental attitude and reception. He had been laboring with Dr. Goodell, then of New Britain, and elsewhere in that region, and was passing through Saybrook to take the night-boat to New York, and having a little time to spare he as usual paid his respects to the minister to inquire concerning the spiritual condition of the place. When he left it was with the promise that if the Tract Society would so arrange it he would come and work with me. I directed him to the boat, but hardly had I closed the door than it occurred to me that I had not shown him the attention belonging to the courier of the King, and that I ought to see him further on his way. Hastily donning my out-door attire, I started after and overtook him about half way to the wharf, which was something like a mile away.

"My heart burned within me while we talked together on the road. I took occasion to introduce him to several whom I met, even stopping two or three wagons

14

for the purpose. To every one he gave a word in season, and most of them wore a puzzled look at this Philip starting up beside their chariots among the desert sand-heaps of Saybrook Point. As some time would elapse before the boat would sail, I left him at the Point and returned home. But these waiting hours were not wasted ones, for not a few laborers and loungers heard the Gospel from his lips even there.

"He was detailed by the Society to work in Saybrook, and made his first appearance in our church on Sabbath morning, November 10th. After the sermon he arose in the midst of the congregation to say a few words by way of greeting and preparation for what he was there to undertake. His movement was so unexpected and so unprecedented in that staid old community, his appearance so plain, his speech so searching, that the general impression was unfavorable. Many afterwards confessed that it took them a long while to get over their prejudice. Possibly the time and mode were not well chosen. Mr. Vassar always contended that he was best adapted to personal effort. But the real 'offence' was that he spoke to Christian professors in such an uncompromising way about their duty, and in such a startling way about their state, that every one whose heart was not honest with itself, or whose peace was a false one, was sure to be stung and irritated.

"As he went through the town I was greatly interested to observe his progress as a kind of touch-stone. He was a veritable sword of the Spirit, discerning the thoughts and intents of the heart and laying bare its secret. The 'poor in spirit' were sure to be revealed. I think he could hardly have encountered more odium and opposition anywhere, especially among the members of the churches. Many of my own people regarded him with great disfavor. The part of the town which had once been the source and centre of revival work, but which had fallen into formalism and routine, was the part in which he found least sympathy and encouragement. Those parts, on the contrary, which were regarded as the most hopeless and God-forsaken, were those where he was most welcome and successful. The poor and prodigal felt the beatings of his great heart as seeker for souls. The most unexpected people in every rank of life 'took' to him, and there were equally unexpected cases of revulsion or dislike. I said that his first public appearance in Saybrook was November 10th. Really it was on the 9th, for on that evening, at his request, I rallied a little group in my parlor to pray. These brethren were completely won to him and to the work. Had there been time to gather a larger number that night, his sudden apparition in the guise of an Elijah in our decorous church the next day might have produced a different effect.

"On Sunday afternoon and evening Mr. Vassar attended all the Sunday-schools and prayer-meetings he could reach. During the week he attended and addressed the district schools. One young man who was teaching declared that he would not allow it, but the old veteran stormed the castle and took possession.

He was a big child everywhere, and could sway and win a group of children at his will.

"On Monday morning he started out, with his districts and families all designated, and began to button-hole every one he met with the characteristic question, 'Are you sure that you have been born again?' As I was able I went with him. Some remarkable scenes took place. We saw a young man chopping wood in his back-yard. We stepped across the road and Uncle John plied him with sword thrusts. The effect was such that he felt prayer was needed, and there by the fence, the youth on one side and we on the other, we took off our hats and prayed. The young man was one of the converts soon.

"At a store we found another young man alone. He found himself cornered, and submitted to the interview with an ill grace, and a sort of dazed look but he, too, quickly came to regard that interview with a very different mind.

"At another place—the post-office I think it was —a group was assembled around the stove. He there knelt and prayed and called on me to follow. The town was soon in a blaze over it, and not all of fire from above.

"We had a season of great quickening and many were converted to the Lord. I regard this work, how-ever, as chiefly valuable for its preparatory, and I might almost say revolutionary, effect. That fallow soil needed just such a sub-soil plow, and I had calculat-ed on it when I engaged him to come. It was a hard, fight, but the question was settled. The whole theory of religion and policy of work were changed from routine to revivalism, and the fruits have been ripening and been gathered ever since.

"What prodigous labor the good man did! He did not realize it himself. Tramp, tramp, from dawn to dark, with such a continuous draft upon his nervous vigor and vitality. I have often marvelled that he held out so long. Oh, how rich I have always felt in the special love and recognition of this great and saintly soul. My children loved him dearly and remember him to this day. There is one tune he used to sing which we call 'Vassar' still. The words he used to put to it were, 'Alas! and did my Saviour bleed.' There was a Catholic woman who would not listen to him or take a tract from his hand, but she did finally suffer him to sing. And to this tune, whose proper name I do not know, he raised the verse:

'But drops of grief can ne'er repay
The debt of love I owe,'

and at its close she was utterly subdued and ultimately became a true Christian. Her experience she used to sum up in the words, Ah those drops of grief, those drops of grief—I couldn't get over them.'

"Perhaps I ought to add one incident showing that Uncle John was capable not only of heroic treatment, but of righteous indignation where the circumstances of the case required it. At a house where we had been holding a neighborhood prayer-meeting one night a man was visiting who was a stranger to us all. As he

*14**

was one who remained at the close of the service Uncle John approached him with his tender earnestness and searching questions. But the man in a dogged and discourteous way opposed a flat denial to every statement made, especially those touching his accountability and danger. I shall never forget the change which came over Uncle John's manner. He rose to a Sinaitic attitude above the wretched caviller, and his captious and blasphemous speech, as if for the moment he was wielding the divine thunderbolts, then suddenly softening into an almost equally awful tenderness he fairly dragged him to the mercy-seat, and called on us to pray. Whether the fellow was savingly affected or not I cannot tell, as he left the place the following day, but he was morally cowed that night, and crouched speechless before Uncle John.

"I have been privileged to labor with him and to know of his labors in all parts of our country, and I never knew any one of such absolute singleness of aim. I confess that, above all men, he has been to me an inspiration, an evidence of Christianity, and an instructor in direct, personal, and practical work in saving souls. My eyes are moist with tender sorrow, as I write. But I am glad that this worn-out veteran of Christ, whose body was literally a living sacrifice for thirty years, has been mustered out. How sweetly his weather-beaten, toil-worn body sleeps and rests. How joyfully has his spirit opened its eyes upon Him "whom not having seen he loved." And how great the works which follow him none may know till the resurrection.

"Whenever we met he took me in his arms as a father would a son. He once took me in his arms before a depot full of people. I happened to be at the station to meet a train, and whom should I see devouring a hasty lunch, but Uncle John. I hailed him. With fork and sandwich in mid-air he responded and gave me a hug, and then began with rapid inquiries about the work in Saybrook, and statements concerning his recent labors elsewhere. He forgot all about his lunch, and it was with difficulty I could prevent his being left behind by the train. He had to give me one more hug after the cars began to move, so that he barely scrambled with my help upon the platform at imminent risk of his life. And there he stood nodding and gesticulating till out of sight. He was not only one of the most holy and consecrated of men, but one of the most original and attractive."

Rev. J. W. Tuck, now of Middletown, Conn., tells of labor at Jewett City, in the same State, in connection with the Congregational church there.

"He came to my house on Saturday evening, November 29th, 1873. The way had been measurably prepared among us by an increased number of meetings, and a prevalent expectation of coming good. The next day he listened to the usual preaching in the morning, and in the afternoon the order of the service was left chiefly in his hands. After the reading of a few verses from the sixtieth chapter of Isaiah and brief comments thereon by the pastor, he came forward and in earnest words falling from lips touched as with a living coal addressed the church for thirty minutes, exhorting them to let their light shine and live above the world. He then proposed that they should publicly renew their covenant vows by coming out into seats which he indicated. The request at first seemed injudicious. The congregation was a most conservative one, the proposition was unexpected, and the man who made it was almost unknown. There was a moment of painful suspense, a silence that could almost be felt. Then a pew door near the front swung open, and one family walked out and complied with the request. Another and another followed until the desired separation was complete; then to both parts of his audience were addressed other ringing words, and so the first meeting closed with tokens of good. In the evening a large assembly met in our conference room. The meeting was remarkable for its solemnity, but no new demonstrations on the part of saint or sinner were proposed. The next night there were greater numbers still, and a deeper interest could be read on every face. It was at this time that many of the new gospel songs began among my people to be introduced. Uncle John was a sweet singer in Israel, and those pieces known as 'Wondrous Love,' 'Sweet By and By,' 'Whiter than Snow,' and many like them he rang out with marvellous effect, and they will be associated with his name and work for a long time to come by the hundreds who first heard them from his lips.

"On this second evening five rose for prayer. The next night fifteen thus responded to the invitation, and now the revival broadened and deepened, overcoming opposition, or holding it in check, till scores had been converted to Christ.

"The special meetings continued only two weeks though they were kept up partially all the winter, but forty were added to our membership and the whole body lifted up to a high plane of Christian life.

"The name of Uncle John to the young people of my former charge—and I might say to the elders also —is to this day an inspiration, and his memory is a sweet savor never to be lost."

In the course of his evangelistic labors he entered the town of Otis, in Western Massachusetts, and what happened there let Rev. O. L. Leonard, who spent a week with him on that ground, tell.

"It was a cold dark time spiritually when Uncle John arrived. The pastor was feeling much disheartened, and said to him, 'The place is dead, the church is dead, we are all dead; if you can do anything to help us, do it.' Uncle John went out and began to visit. It was right in the heat of summer, and the people, who were mostly farmers, were busy in the fields. 'No time for a revival now;' that was what they said right to his face.

"He believed that the dry bones could live. The church was opened. It was soon filled. Soon the old cry began to be heard, 'What shall I do to be saved?' and the town was shaken by the mighty power of God. About fifty souls were converted in that farming region right in the heat of summer."

Another who was led to Christ during these meetings reports them more at length.

"For many days after coming to Otis Centre, Uncle John saw almost no result from the efforts put forth. Even his courage seemed somewhat shaken, but not enough to make him let go or even relax endeavor. And presently the blessing came like the rush of many waters. The writer well remembers the evening when the first token of giving way appeared. The meeting had been more constrained than usual, and Uncle John was perceptibly cast down. Before it closed one arose and requested prayers. The effect was electrical. From that point concern took the place of apathy, and salvation moved right on. The whole town was shaken, and ultimately the towns around. It was spoken of by the religious press as the midsummer revival, and the scene of the farmers working in the hay field all day and attending the meeting at evening day after day certainly was wonderful.

"The tact of Uncle John seemed almost supernatural. Many instances of his unerring judgment in approaching people might be given, but two or three must suffice. One man had arranged for an argument with Uncle John if he should be addressed, which he felt sure would settle the whole case. Uncle John gave him no chance to speak. He came up all smiling, invited the man to meeting, told him he knew his duty, and before an answer could be given was off. The man began to think, and was led to Christ.

"Another had arranged for a ridiculous scene if

Uncle John came. He did not go near the man, and this unlooked-for way of disconcerting the carefully laid scheme set reflection working, and this man and his wife both turned to the Lord.

"All too soon came the time for him to leave our vicinity, but his influence remained, and for a long time yet his name will be revered in Otis, and his memory be a power."

From North Blandford, where he wrought the following summer, these reminiscences come.

"I was at work in my garden in the summer of 1875, when I observed an odd little man walking rapidly toward the parsonage, and thinking him to be some book agent I continued my work. As he came up he said in a pleasant voice, 'Watchman, what of the night?' I replied, 'Glory to God, the morning cometh:' He extended to me his hand, and I knew John Vassar. He was taken at once into the parsonage and quickly into all our hearts.

"The work contemplated during the few days he could remain was fully discussed; and here he exhibited that trait of Christian character which was everywhere so manifest, his humility. He began his labors with me Sunday, July 18th. It was a pleasant day, and many came to hear the strange man of whom so much had been said. He read the first psalm and gave a beautiful exposition of it, showing how mighty he was in the Word of God. All through the week services were kept up and the awakening was great. Those who never came to the sanctuary were hunted to their hiding places and led out. Stumbling blocks that seemed in the way were removed, and though his stay was short he prepared the way for the rich revival that followed. In our community he was emphatically a John the Baptist, sent to prepare the way of the Lord."

Of these labors in Western Massachusetts Rev. George L. Ruberg, then a pastor in that section, also gives a report. "Uncle John's introduction to this part of the State was through the kindly interest of Homer Merriam, Esq., of Springfield, who was so deeply concerned about the low state of religion prevailing that he felt constrained to assume the expense of evangelical labor for the field. Arrangements were made for Uncle John to visit Otis in May, 1874. A series of meetings were held in the Congregational Church, and many of the leading citizens of the village and surrounding community were led to Christ.

"During the work the hotel was even opened for prayer-meetings, and the power of God was most graciously displayed.

"So manifest was the good accomplished that Mr. Merriam determined to send Uncle John on a summer campaign amid the Berkshire hills; so after leaving Otis, Sandisfield secured his services for a week. In this town there had not been for a long time any general revival of religion, and there was not in any of the churches a resident male member under thirty years of age, though we had a larger number of young men living there than in any town around.

"Uncle John's visit here had been but briefly announced, yet the church at Montville village was ready to receive him. I went with my own carriage to meet him, and found him out calling still, so anxious was he to improve even the last moment of his stay. Hardly had we finished dinner before he said, 'Are there no places we can visit yet this afternoon?' The inquiry impressed me, for it was now three o'clock or later, and I had expected he would want to rest so as to be ready for the meeting at night. We immediately started out. Our first call was at the post-office. Found two persons beside the postmaster in. One was a Christian, and the others were not. All were tenderly addressed; then with his hand resting on the counter and standing he offered a short but most fervent prayer. I shall never forget that scene, and what subsequently occurred.

"One lady on whom we called was considered a woman of devout piety. In answer to the question, 'Do you love Jesus?' She said, rather despondently,

Not half so well as I ought.' 'Dear sister,' said Uncle John, 'I wish you would tell me how I can love Him more?'

"From the first day of his coming the revival went steadily on. Although for a farming community it was the busiest season of the year, none tried to excuse 'themselves from being seen. Men not at all in sympathy with religious things would lay down the hoe in the field, or suspend any other labor, and go into the house for conversation and prayer. Uncle John seemed unwilling to pass any house.

15

"The last night he was in our place, as the bell was ringing and we were on our way to church, we noticed a group of men on the steps of a store opposite the post-office. Among them was a loud-mouthed and low-mouthed scoffer. He beckoned from the crowd, saying, 'Captain, I want to speak to you?'

'Do you mean *me*?' asked Uncle John. "Yes,' was the reply. Uncle John told me to go on and open the meeting, and promptly crossed the street where the blasphemer stood. The man's first remark was that if Uncle John did not leave the place within twenty-four hours he would 'give him a thrashing.' Uncle John kindly but fearlessly replied that his engagements would compel him to go the following day, but that if the arrangements were not already made he would certainly remain. Some of the best citizens witnessed the interview and were deeply impressed, when Uncle John, taking the abusive fellow's hand, plead with him and prayed till he was subdued to perfect silence. A number came over to our meeting that night for the first time, declaring that if they had any moral influence they wanted to cast it on that side.

Among those who so sought to express their opinion of this transaction was the postmaster of the village and another prominent citizen, both of whom were converted; and another who had previously led a reckless life in relating his experience said that his conviction of sin started when he heard Uncle John so attacked. That exhibition of depravity convinced him of the exceeding 'sinfulness of sin.' Satan sometimes blunders fearfully. That night and there he overleaped himself.

"For months Sandisfield, Colebrook, Conn., Lee, Tyringham, and Monterey felt the effect of Uncle John's incessant labors, or perhaps we should put it—the power of God. He who called himself 'legs for Baxter and Bunyan' was a voice for Homer Merriam as well. The accessions to the churches following his labors were more than three hundred, and the man will be lovingly remembered in many a household for years to come. Even the children of tender age will long remember one who so much loved them and whom they so much loved."

Of this same memorable summer, and of this same vicinity, let a Christian woman speak, mentioning briefly a special case or two.

"In one family in Otis there were nine conversions, and most of them have been earnest workers in the good cause ever since. In another there were four brought to accept of Christ, and hardly one household was there some member of which did not come to sing the wonders of redeeming grace. Often I heard Uncle John say, 'I can never doubt any more, so wonderful have been the answers to prayer.'

Only once do I remember seeing him introduced to a stranger to whom he did not say something about the great salvation. This one was an elderly lady who happened to be in the room when he called on business. He left the house and was perhaps as far as the gate when the omission occurred to him, and back again he came and talked with her and prayed."

"Lost for want of a word!
A word that *you* might have spoken—
Who knows what eyes may be dim,
Or hearts be aching or broken?

Go, scatter beside all waters,
Nor sicken at hope deferred;
Let never a soul by thy dumbness
Be lost for want of a word!"

"Mr. Vassar absorbed himself for the time being with the individual he was talking with, and by some happy gift made each one feel that he was deeply interested in his particular case. And there was no pretence in this. He took in rapidly the interesting points in any stranger's condition, with great tact drew out the religious state, and urged with impressiveness the importance of being at peace with God. The secret of this was that his whole heart was in the work of winning souls to discipleship with Christ, and the ground of his interest in others was, therefore, not, as so much it is with most of us, personal and worldly considerations, but eminently Christian and arising out of his habitual prayerfulness. It was, therefore, easy for him to make even a stranger see that he was cordially interested in his religious welfare. He followed closely the prudential maxims of Matt. 10, worked hard all the year round, and was manifestly denying himself much of what most men count essential to comfort. Loving, faithful, unobtrusive, without title or ordination, he preached the gospel like his divine Master, wherever he found a weary heart and ready ear. He was an evangelist of whom all pastors spoke well; for he knew his work and never aimed to go beyond it."

Another Christian woman tells of a man in Sandisfield seventy-four years of age, profane, and of drinking habits, who declared that he had never felt himself a sinner till Uncle John got hold of his hand and began to plead with him. For days he passed through agony of mind much like that which uncle John himself experienced, but at last came into the peace of Christ and demonstrated the genuineness of his hope afterward by an upright life.

Of his labors in Boston and vicinity Rev. Drs. Gordon and Fulton will elsewhere tell. Enough to say just here that his sterling worth and efficient services were recognized and appreciated by cultured Christian men as well as by a humbler class, and that to their homes and churches he was welcomed as a brother beloved in the Lord, and a laborer esteemed for his work's sake. Henry F. Durant, the founder of Wellesley College, in inviting him to his elegant home for a week, said to a mutual friend, "I consider myself more honored to entertain this man of God than to have a king for my guest."

In the Charlestown district, where for two winters he aided different pastors, one of them already quoted says, "The meetings we held were foretastes of heaven. Uncle John was at his best. He had great physical infirmities, but he rose above them, as he often said, "by mighty faith and prayer.' Oh, what days those were! Would God we might see their like

15*

again. Hundreds entered into covenant with Christ and His church."

Of a week spent at Keyport, N. J., Rev. J. K. Manning, with whom he labored, has this to say:

We were in the midst of a powerful revival when he came, and his first words after learning our condition were, 'I am not needed here. My chief work is among churches that are measurably cold or dead.' With difficulty he was persuaded to remain, and with the deacons go from house to house. The service he rendered in this way was grand.

"For three characteristics especially he is remembered here.

"First, his resort to prayer when met by cavilling or gainsaying tongues, and his readiness to plead with men, and for men, in any place, and in every circumstance.

"Second. His persistent holding of the penitent and inquiring soul to the promises of God as the means and source of comfort. He was the most faithful to the Word of God of any man I ever knew.

"Third. The impression made on all minds that doing good was the mission of his life. Many speak of him yet as the man who knew nothing excepting the seeking and saving of souls."

To another New Jersey pastor anxious to secure his services for a few days he writes:

DEAR BROTHER LOVE:

"I have your kind letter, and rejoice to hear of the salvation of souls at Croton. God grant the work may be deep and widespread. I would come and help you if I could, but I have been four months with Dr. Tyng, who has received more than seven hundred this year into the membership of his church, and am now engaged elsewhere for a season. My heart is with you."

The "tent work" of Dr. Tyng's referred to above he will tell us of elsewhere. One who was with Uncle John all through it says, "Let me speak of one little prayer-meeting in the street. After the tent service one night a group of us were returning home together, our hearts full of joy over the scenes of grace and mercy from which we had just come, and on the corner of Thirty-fourth Street and Madison Avenue we stopped beside an iron railing and began to sing and pray. It was a precious season, and the wandering street sweepers dropped their brooms and gathered quietly around, as under the stars declaring the glory of God in creation we sang of His greater glory in redemption through Christ our Lord."

Rev. S. L. Bowler, of Machias, Maine, now secured Uncle John's services for some of the more destitute regions of that State. In a single county there were a score of churches that had no pastor, most of them being too feeble to maintain one. The Maine Missionary Society cordially co-operated with the lay evangelist, and the results everywhere else witnessed were here quickly seen and felt.

From one of the churches thus visited and blest a Christian man sends these lines:

"His labors here were crowned with great success. The church was quickened; souls were saved; every house in the place I think was visited, and he conversed with nearly every person in the town. One young sea captain who was evidently failing with consumption interested Uncle John very much. He had not been married long, and neither he nor his wife had the Christian's trust. Oh, how he did entreat them! and even when praying elsewhere, especially at our family devotions, he would break out with 'Oh, God, bless the captain and his wife.' The prayer was fully answered. Both were happily converted. He died soon after, and she has followed him now to the other side.

"While he was with us our only child first manifested an interest in religious things, and the very walls of our house seem to have been made sacred by his many prayers.

"I can never forget our last interview. He had gone on board the steamer after commending us tenderly to the Lord and bidding us good-by, when I had occasion again to see him at nearly eleven o'clock at night. Quietly I went to his berth thinking he might be asleep, and found him repeating over the names of persons in our place. He said he was doing it that he might carry them individually to God in prayer. As the parting hand was finally given he said, "I am an old man, and shall probably go before you, but by the grace of God I shall expect to meet you again in heaven.' His prediction has proved correct. God grant his hope may find its realization."

From another source these reflections come:

"I cannot help thinking, that if Uncle John had lived in Galilee about A. D. 30, he would have been, either one of the twelve, or else of the seventy, and quite as companionable with Jesus as any of them. As it is, I doubt whether his apostolic namesake loved his Saviour any better.

"One instance of his spiritual insight and modesty I recall. Rev. Jacob Knapp was laboring in a series of revival meetings in Chicago, and Uncle John was there. Day after day the mighty evangelist preached, and although crowds thronged the church still there were no manifest fruits. No one sought the Lord. No one asked for prayer. It had not been so before. Had God forgotten to be gracious? The enemies of Christ only mocked. The evangelist in his trouble went to see Uncle John, and asked of him the explanation of the mystery. 'Why is it,' said Elder Knapp, 'that I seem to be laboring in vain, and spending my strength for naught?' About that time the evangelist had bought a farm containing sixteen hundred acres, and probably his mind was somewhat 'of the earth earthy.' Uncle John heard his story through, and then said in his modest way, Dear brother Knapp, it is not for the Lord's poor dust to attempt to give you any light, but *I have been wondering how one of the Lord's diamonds could shine with sixteen hundred acres of earth on it.'* The evangelist took the gentle wise rebuke, the earth was shaken from off the diamond, and the light so shone that God was glorified in the conversion of a multitude of souls."

The following account of one of the most extensive ingatherings of souls in which for the last year or two of life he shared, is from the pen of Mr. J. C. Tiffany, who was with him through it, and in later labors in Greene County, N. Y.

"About the first of February, 1877, a revival of God's work was progressing in the M. E. church of Coxsackie, N. Y. Its pastor, Rev. Gideon Draper, becoming weary under prolonged efforts, requested the writer to see if he could not obtain some help from abroad. I arrived in New York in the evening, and attended service at the Church of the Holy Trinity, Dr. S. H. Tyng, Jr., Rector. There I heard Uncle John Vassar pray with great unction and power. I applied to Dr. Tyng for aid, and out of the largeness of his heart he arranged to send his then assistant, Rev. Mr. Humpstone, for a few days, and Uncle John for a longer time. They went up to Coxsackie at once. The pastor and official board were at a store waiting to meet us. They began to lay plans of work. Uncle John took off his hat and said, "Let us pray about it.' This was something new to us, and the customers in the store had whereof to talk.

"Before night came he had struck in among the people in his usual way, and many were saying that we had got a crazy man to help us. He called right up to meeting time, stopping only to get a hasty meal. The effect was seen the first evening in an increased attendance. Seeing the backwardness of many Christians, a consecration meeting among them was proposed. It was a season never to be forgotten. Coldness melted away, denominational lines were broken down, and the people of God were ready for their work. A daily noon prayer-meeting was started. Christians of all names came into it. Many young men came in and turned to God. Strong men bowed themselves at Jesus' feet, and many hardened sinners found a Saviour. It was no unusual thing to have from eight to fifteen conversions in a single day. Some answers to prayer were wonderful.

"The room in which the meeting was held was offered by a man who held a license to sell liquor, and who kept a grocery. The offer was accepted, and the young men soon had it ready for occupation. The meeting was crowded. A few remarks were made in regard to Jesus at the grave of Lazarus, when he said, 'Jesus wept.' A power came which made every head of Christian and sinner bow on the seat before it. For a few moments an awful stillness followed which was broken by the cries for mercy from the son of the man who had given the room; then one of his companions, then others. The room could not accommodate to bow in prayer, so the ladies were left in that, and the men sought places in neighboring houses. It was a scene for Coxsackie. Fathers went through the streets with children, sons almost of age crying and weeping, and others praying for mercy. Each day he selected some brother to visit with him from house to house. Many were the souls thus savingly reached.

"After four weeks thus spent at the Landing we went to the upper village, and the First Reformed Church opened its doors for the service. The work of salvation started the first day. Old difficulties were reconciled, and estranged neighbors or brethren made one. Old grudges and animosities, which had gone so far as to prevent those sharing them from speaking to each other, were swept away. At one of the noon prayer-meetings a divine power fell on the people such as Uncle John himself confessed that he had never seen displayed.

"On one of his visits he came with his companions to a house where there was a family party of seven adults, non-professors. He soon had the strong men and women bowed in prayer; all promised to seek salvation. They were all rejoicing in a very few days, and as the result, two of the number are now deacons in the church, and all happy in the Lord. Members of different churches came in to help, and, young and old, all pressed forward longing for a fresh baptism of the Holy Ghost. Uncle John knew no differences. He was working for souls for the Master, and all recognized his zeal.

The apparent result of the work was that over three hundred were added to the churches there, while some joined elsewhere. More than one hundred of this number were young business men between eighteen and thirty years of age, the most of whom are active working Christians still. Schoolhouse meetings were started in the country round about, which are yet kept up, and in which conversions are from time to time occurring now, resulting from seed then sown.

"Many who were then converted have already entered into rest. They have again met the dear old man, but this time at the feet of the Master, where they will part no more. We who remain are going on to join the heavenly throng saved by grace divine."

These attacks "all along the line" were coming to an end. There is but one more that we shall mention or give the details of in this chapter. It was at Greenville, Greene County, N. Y., where it was made, and Rev. W. P. Gibson reports it.

"My first impression on seeing Uncle John at my gate was that he was some old wide-awake farmer turned book-agent, who had come to the parsonage having a special axe to grind; but as he had been at my house once when I was absent, my family recognized him, and he was soon perfectly at home. Seven weeks we spent together travelling those hills, talking, preaching, praying; and it was nearly his last work here below.

"On one occasion he was seen praying with a group of men along the road, and was published as an escaped lunatic in our village paper. Sometimes his kind approaches were repulsed, but *never, so far as I am aware, by a non-professor of religion.* In one or two instances nominal Christians declined having any conversation with him, or any prayer offered in their homes, asserting that they belonged to the church and had no need of such service."

"When introduced to any one he lost no time in pressing home that all important question, "My dear son!' or 'My dear daughter, have you been born again?' and if there was any hesitancy, his well-worn testament was opened spontaneously to the words 'Ye must be born again.' And then he would graphically describe the interview between Christ and Nicodemus, or picture the scene among the bitter Israelites when Moses lifted up the serpent (typical of Christ) for the gaze of the dying. And every brief interview closed with prayer, by himself or the 'dear pastor' and sometimes all the praying members of the household were pressed to join, or a trembling soul seeking light was encouraged to put up a short broken petition. On one occasion, a back-slidden sister was tearfully seeking for peace and pardon but could see no light. He saw at once that it was unbelief, and said, 'My dear, you must believe when you pray;' and bid her say over and over, "I do believe, I will believe; help thou my unbelief.' It was not long before peace came. Sometimes the interview occurred on the street; after a few faithful words, off went his hat without warning and a short petition went up to God for a blessing on the message.

"After visiting all day, he would give a detailed account of his visits, calling the name of every member of the families met, and their spiritual condition. He would then kneel and pour out his heart for them, one by one, naming each particular case in his petition. He was quick to detect the secret of a cold and half-hearted profession."

"His modesty forbade his leading the meetings unless specially requested, but his stirring exhortations and moving petitions told upon the audience powerfully at times. I remember a few impassioned appeals that were truly eloquent with lofty and well-expressed thought. His singing too was a great help. Though his voice was somewhat weakened and roughened by age, he sang with the spirit, and his selections invariably fitted the places where they came in. On one occasion we were singing at family worship,

'Oh, why was He there as the bearer of sin
If on Jesus my sin was not laid?'

As the thought took possession of him he exclaimed, 'Sure enough,' and repeating the lines he laughed and wept for very joy.

"Dear Uncle John! his stay with us was like an angel's visit, and we cherish his words and looks in memory, as of one very intimate with Jesus, and dwelling even here "quite on the verge of heaven.' "

During these meetings one who roomed with him many nights says: "At this time he was suffering severely from the disease which caused his death, and the pain at intervals was fearful. During one of these intervals, when he supposed me sleeping, after being up for a while he came back to bed and laid down as carefully as a mother would by her sick child for fear of disturbing me, and then in an underbreath I heard him say, *"Dear Lord, how much better this than sin!"* "

Another, writing of a date perhaps earlier, says. "A little incident occurred which pleased me very much the night he stopped with us. When I went to show him to his room I said on entering it, 'We call this the prophet's chamber. Many ministers have occupied it, but it is doubly hallowed to us since in it our dear old pastor laid off his robe of flesh and went to God.' Uncle John's face fairly beamed with delight as he exclaimed, "Oh, I am so glad to know that there is a passage direct from here to heaven!' "

He was ripening now rapidly. He was soon to see the King in his beauty.

CHAPTER IX.

WEAPONS IN THE FIGHT.

"His was the saint's high faith,
And quenchless Hope's pure glow,
And perfect Charity, which laid
The world's fell tyrant low.
In him the Father shone;
In him the Son o'ercame;
In him the Holy Spirit wrought,
And filled his heart with flame."

IT is exceedingly difficult to analyze what men call personal power. It is easily recognized and readily confessed, but its elements are not easily discovered or described. John Vassar struck blows that fell heavy and cut deep. What were the weapons used? Dropping the figure, what made him the man he was?

Certain constitutional peculiarities probably helped: natural ardor, vivacity, persistency, sympathy, had something to do with the work. We will not leave them altogether out of the account. But the real springs of character were not in these. The palm of the desert, fruitful and beautiful, does not find its supplies in itself. Nor does it find them in the burning, blistering sand out of which it grows. The sources of its life lie deeper down. Far underneath are veins of water at which its rootlets drink and from which they draw up nourishment which keeps the uppermost and outmost leaves fresh and fair when sultry suns are smiting. A consecrated life depends on unseen and eternal sources for what it is and what it gives. Some of Uncle John's characteristics have of necessity been brought in sight, and the secret sources of their strength have been glimpsed as we have gone along. They need, however, to be set in a stronger light, and all eyes turned on them; for the practical effect of this book will be short-lived and superficial unless Christian men can be made to see what are, and must ever be, the elements as well as the sources of personal spiritual power.

Though it may involve more or less repetition, then let the strong points of the man be stated and emphasized, and further illustrated.

Unflinching loyalty to the Lord Jesus Christ, based on an adoring love, was the mainspring to all he was and all he did.

Somebody has said of Arnold of Rugby that "the central fact of his experience was his close, conscious, and ever-realized union and friendship with the Lord Jesus; and that in the ever-flowing fulness of his heart every expression of affection that might pass between earthly friends passed between him and the Divine Man whom as a friend he had in heaven, and to whom with an exhaustless enjoyment he clung." A picture in words this of Uncle John. An irreverent mention of the Saviour's name would cause him keen distress. While we were residing in Lynn, Mass., he made us several flying visits, on one of which a Unitarian gentleman of the city said to him, in a flash of irritation, "Sir, to pay divine honor to this Jesus of Nazareth of whom you talk so much is in my opinion insulting to the Almighty." It was hours before Uncle John got over that. It pained him more than if child or brother had received a cruel thrust.

And he was just as sensitive if there was no recognition of that Name where he thought it ought to have a place. One day he came out of W— Street church, where a noted minister had preached, and with a grieved, disappointed look and a quivering voice he said, "Oh, T–, he never mentioned the name of Jesus once."

And in all this there was not a particle of pretence or cant. This love of Christ was not a fancy or a sentiment. It was a principle, a passion, an abiding motive. It was the antidote against worldliness. It was the incentive to action which this world could not understand, and for which it sometimes had nothing more than scorn. Heavy loads and hard toils grew light when with this affection the heart glowed. Poverty, reproach, death even—what were they but the passing flurries of an April day? Who that was intimate but has heard him say:

> "One smile, one blissful smile of Thine,
> My dearest Lord, outweighs them all."

When they were probing among his shattered ribs for the fatal bullet, the French veteran exclaimed, "A little deeper, and you will find the emperor." In Uncle John's heart the deepest emotion was love for his Saviour. Deeper than the love of home, deeper than the love of kindred, deeper than the love of country, aye deeper than the love of life, was his affection for that Redeemer who had first loved him and given Himself for him. He did not talk so much of heaven as many Christians do. He talked of being with the Lord and like Him. That was his ideal of the coming blessedness.

Out of this attachment grew what was probably the next most prominent feature of his life, and one of the mightiest forces in his work—*his habitual and almost unbroken intercourse with God in prayer.*

A man who came so near a literal compliance with the apostolic charge, "Pray without ceasing," few Christians in these latter days have known. One long his pastor, and longer still his friend, bears testimony on this point that a stranger might think too strong, but every word of which hundreds would indorse.

"He absolutely prayed day and night. Prayed about every thing. Prayed over every thing. Prayed for almost everybody, and prayed with almost everybody whom he met. He prayed when he went out, and when he came in. He prayed before every religious service, and then prayed all the way through it. I have roomed with him night after night, and rarely went to sleep without hearing him at prayer, or awoke without finding him at prayer. He seldom, if ever, came into my house or study that he did not propose a season of prayer, no matter how brief might be the call, or what the errand that brought him there."

His gift in prayer was very remarkable—more remarkable, we think, than his gift of speech, though that was sometimes wonderful, and always of a more than ordinary kind. Several special supplications of his have already been referred to, and prayers very like them others will recall.

William N. Sage, Esq., of Rochester, N. Y., speaks of one such which he offered in that city a dozen years ago. The First Baptist Church had just finished a "memorial chapel" on Lake Avenue, and before its formal dedication Uncle John and the late Deacon Oren Sage—a kindred spirit—went into it alone, and there on bended knees wrestled with God that His awakening and converting Spirit might so fill those courts that of many of the finally redeemed it might be said, " This man and that were born there." He further adds that most signally and graciously God answered that request, and by displays of His salvation made the place of His feet glorious.

In a prayer-meeting he was a host. If a spirit of dulness or heaviness pervaded it, somehow it seemed, as he began to wrestle, to be lifted off. One of the members of his own church who has already been quoted tells what animation his simple presence gave to the little company that met there in the usual devotional meetings of the week.

"He was often sent home to rest by the Tract Society, but before he would go home even he would stop into the prayer-meeting of his church if it happened to be going on. If we did not see him enter we would quickly know that he was there. Oh, how he would wrestle for the dear old church in which he was born again! Then how he would recount recent wonders of redeeming grace, keeping himself all the time in the background and giving God the glory. No matter how truthfully we might have been singing

> "Hosannas languish on our tongues,
> And our devotion dies,"

It seemed as we listened to him as good to be there as it was to the apostles to be on the mount of transfiguration, and the Lord granted us such revelations of Himself as made our place of prayer something like that hilltop for radiance."

Few phrases are more common among Christian men than this, "the *privilege* of prayer;" but it is greatly to be feared that many who use it would more correctly represent their own personal feeling if they were to say "the *drudgery* of prayer." At least an honest conscience would compel them to say that it was a dull duty; uninviting often, and sometimes positively irksome, and engaged in as much to keep a sense of obligation quiet as for any thing else. Now to John Vassar prayer was a privilege, a blessed privilege, and a real deep delight. It was a lament of the prophet over the degeneracy of God's people, "None *stirreth himself up* to take hold of Thee." That is, devotion was a droning, drawling thing. There was no holy energy about the exercise. This was not true of Uncle John. He seemed to know the meaning of those mysterious expressions, "Praying in the Holy

Ghost," "With all prayer in the Spirit;" and so his supplications were intense. There was a specific object to attain. Coming to the throne of grace was not a romance or a pious farce. He could not approach it "with easiness of desire." He could not tamely beg. There were "deep-swelling sensibilities," as Dr. Phelps calls them, to be relieved. It was deep calling unto deep.

Whether the repeated instances given us of his praying along the roads, and in stores and shops, are to be commended and held up for our example, is a question concerning which good men may disagree. Circumstances would have to decide the case. In many instances it might be a perfectly proper thing to do; at least a perfectly proper thing for *him*. We should not feel warranted to urge such a course on all. A brother pastor near us voices about our own opinion in the case: "It seems to me that it would be a fatal mistake for many to venture on the ground which Uncle John trod with so much success. Very few could say or do what he did without making 'a mess' of it. There must be the man, the character; so much depends on that. The tone, the manner, the evident sincerity, may command respect in one case where it would be very offensive in another. What is heroic boldness in one man might be insolent rudeness in another, and do vastly more harm than good."

Obviously enough, the besetting sin of good men today is not to "violate the proprieties" in their efforts to save souls; so while not insisting that Uncle

John's example is a model in every particular for all who would win the wandering to Christ, the question may well be asked, and seriously pondered, whether we are not in danger, by our over-nice notions concerning means and methods, of letting men perish whom we have been commanded to pull out of the fire.

Interwoven with these other qualities there was in Uncle John a *mighty faith.*

No place and no case seemed too hard or too hopeless for him to grapple with. Forbidding circumstances and a gloomy outlook never shook his trust nor tied his tongue. Indeed, he saw no gloomy outlook, for he did not look *out* so much as *up.* If asked what the prospect was in any direction, he would have said, with Adoniram Judson, "As bright as the promises of God." He did not believe simply in the God of ages ago. He believed in the God of today. He could not be persuaded that the wonder-working Spirit finished His operations at Pentecost. He could not be convinced that the supernatural was no longer to be looked for. He could see no reason why the modern Saul of Tarsus should not be as sharply called and as suddenly turned as the ancient persecuting zealot was. When going on what others regarded as "a forlorn hope," he would go into the closet and beg for a special anointing, an enduement of power from on high, and then with a deepened confidence start out. "One day he went to call on a lady whose husband was a skeptic and a bitter opposer of religion. The man saw him entering the gate, and stepping to the door, said, 'You are coming here to pray with my wife, I presume. Now let me tell you I don't allow any prayer in this house. Leave at once, and never show your face here again.' Uncle John hesitated a moment, then left, and going to his stopping-place plead long and earnestly for help to reach that case. Rising from his knees, and 'nothing doubting,' he went straight back to the house from which he had been less than an hour before repulsed. The man again met him, and after a moment's parleying told him that if he would not pray he might come in. Uncle John refused to make any such promise, but nevertheless got in. An urgent message from God was soon ringing in the unbeliever's ears, and before the interview ended, humbled and subdued he was bowing by the side of Uncle John listening to supplications for his own salvation."

Again and again, when assured that a contemplated effort would be fruitless, that it would be the sinking of a bucket in a dry well, and the bringing of nothing up, he would beg the privilege of trying. He would get a church or a school-house open, and then explore the region to invite the people out. Almost invariably a revival would commence. Often God would triumph gloriously. Converts would be multiplied. Dull churches or dull Christians would get aglow. There would be apostolic work because it was underlaid and pushed with apostolic faith.

It would be foolish, and even false, to say that religiously there are no hard fields and no hard souls.

17

There are both. When Christ appointed the Seventy, the record is that He sent them "into every city and place whither *He himself would come.*" It sometimes looks now as if there were places where He did not come. They seem as dry, spiritually, as those mountains of Gilboa would have been, literally, had David's desire been granted and neither rain nor dew had dropped upon their slopes. There are hearts that do appear almost unimpressible. Warnings and appeals, no matter how faithful or how pungent, seem to glide off like hail from a slated roof, and leave traces as faint and few behind.

In such circumstances one needs the faith Elijah had when, with the brazen skies hanging over Carmel, he bade Ahab hurry homeward before the rain should overtake. Uncle John had it in an eminent degree. He never forgot what grace had done for him. He believed it could do as much for any other man.

His *acquaintance with the Bible was very intimate and thorough,* every promise and penalty and precept and prophecy being apparently at his command.

To him Scripture was the one standard of Christian truth. To its teachings nothing was to be added; from its decisions there could be no appeal. In dealing with errorists, the only question he would allow himself to look at was, What has God said? The moment any thing like quibbling or cavilling was heard, out would come his well-worn Testament, and text after text would be turned to till captious lips were closed. The inspired Word was the book he studied most. It was to him exactly what it claims to be—"the sword of the Spirit;" and what was the hilt, and what the blade, and how to get hold of the one and smite with the other, was what he sought to know. The authenticity of Scripture he never stopped to argue. He boldly assumed that, and then by its utterances every opinion must be hewed and squared.

We shall make a great mistake, however, if we get the impression that he studied the Bible chiefly as a controversialist. It was not so much an armory whence to draw weapons as a well whence to draw waters for a thirsty soul. The daily draught was a refreshing and delight. Out of the divine testimonies he drew help and comfort in every case. If he found himself after a day of hard labor with half an hour of spare time before an evening meal or meeting, he would seize the inspired volume as eagerly as he would a letter from home, and some sweet promise, read perhaps for the thousandth time, would bring a smile to his face, and put audible praise upon his tongue.

Nor was it only the doctrinal and devotional portions of Scripture that he pored over and enjoyed. The prophecies were a mine of wealth that he dug into as a treasure-seeker might dig into beds of precious ore. Along their dimmest passages, and in their obscurest recesses, he traced the footprints of his Lord. Christ coming or Christ to come again, and the fortunes of His cause between the first and second advents, he saw promised and presaged at every step. And it is but just to say that while all might not accept his interpretations of prophecy, or the views to which they led, none could doubt that his knowledge of their letter was extensive and exact.

This exhaustive acquaintance with God's word could not fail to make itself felt. Men saw that he was not dogmatically insisting on his own notions or impressions or conceits. They were asked not to listen to him or to believe him, but the message which God had sent. The very reverence with which he treated the message showed that he regarded it as God-sent. And when he came with comfort, though the manner might be human, the matter was divine. It was not the weak, uncertain words of earth he spoke; it was the strong, infallible words of heaven. Such utterances must carry weight. What man may think or feel is perhaps of little consequence; what God says is of vital importance to a thoughtful soul.

Perhaps the quality that would be noticed soonest and most deeply felt was the man's burning *zeal*. It glowed in the awful earnestness with which he pressed his personal appeals. We use the word "awful" advisedly and deliberately, for no other would be as exact.

A writer in the *Watchman*, of Boston, refers to it in this story—a story so characteristic that any one who knew Uncle John would have inferred that he was the man referred to had no name been given.

"While laboring with me a few years since in Boston, he wished to call on a Christian gentleman who was living at one of our fashionable boarding-houses.

A young friend of mine who went with him to show him the place reported what occurred. While waiting in the parlor to be shown to the gentleman's room, he opened conversation with a very fashionable and proud-looking lady who was sitting in the room. With great concern he began to urge the necessity of the new birth and immediate acceptance of Christ upon her. She was thunderstruck, and protested that she did not believe in any of those things. Then followed a most fervent appeal, texts of Scripture, warnings against rejecting Christ, the certainty of a wrath to come for any found in impenitence, till at last my friend said he was fairly alarmed at the boldness of the assault. Suddenly the gentleman came in for whom he was waiting and called him out. The friend sat watching from behind his newspaper for the effect of the interview. In a moment the lady's husband came in. 'There has been an old man here talking with me about religion,' she said. 'Why did you not shut him up?' he asked gruffly. 'He is one of those persons you *can't* shut up,' was her reply. 'If I had been here,' he said, 'I would have told him very quickly to go about his business.' 'If you had seen him *you would have thought he was about his business,'* was her answer. No truer tribute could be paid to him than that. Never did I see one who could 'close in with a soul,' as the old Puritans used to phrase it, like him."

See the same trait shine out in such an incident as Rev. S. B. Almy, of Mattewan, one of Uncle John's dear friends in the younger ministry, relates.

17*

"In the winter of 1872, while at home on a brief visit from Florida, he spent a few days with the pastor of a Presbyterian Church in his native county. Some began to be concerned about their salvation, and special meetings were appointed at the church. One day the minister was taken ill. There was an appointment out for preaching that very night. Nine miles Uncle John walked through snow and slush to get some one to fill the gap, and then kept on with his calls from house to house to get the people out to hear the Word.

This is the way he spent the vacation given him to rest in! Well might his pastor say on the day of his burial, 'More truthfully than any other man I ever knew he might have said, "the zeal of Thine house hath eaten me up."

"In Uncle John a mind of natural strength and fervency had received a powerful impulse from on high. To him, religious things were not invisible and distant, they were seen and present. His awakened soul accepted Bible truths as living and wonderful realities. Christ's cross and judgment-seat seemed very near, radiant with tender attractions and with awful glories. The curtain concealing futurity had fallen; and from beholding the endless destinies of the righteous and the wicked, he turned to his fellow-men, and earnestly besought them to seek the divine favor and preparation for heaven."

"His practical zeal for God and souls, arising from a vivid realization of the truths of religion, was no temporary flame. Burning with wonderful brightness, and with marvellous fervor, it was the immediate cause of his ceaseless activity.

"His intellect and emotions were stirred. The wisdom of perception was united to the vitalizing gloss of ardent feeling. A man of ordinary capacity, hurled ever forward by burning zeal, will perform more than he of tenfold ability cold and passionless. The most sluggish are moved by the magnetic power of a master-mind stirred to its depths by a mighty purpose. It was zeal that possessed David Livingstone, and drove him into the unknown regions of Africa—that held him in Africa until he died on bended knee, hugging Africa to his heart in dying prayer. It is not when man has zeal, but when zeal has the man, filling, controlling, inspiring him, that success is sure."

More than this, Uncle John possessed remarkable *persistency of purpose.*

Zeal is sometimes flashy and fitful. It is good for a dash, but not for a siege. It takes hold well, but it does not keep hold. In the heathery turf of Scotland there is a plant whose roots run but a little distance and then terminate as squarely as if they had been chopped off. The superstitious country folks around assert that great medicinal virtue originally dwelt in these roots, and that to destroy it the great enemy of man once bit them off. A quaint fancy, of course, but something very like it is the fact in many a life. Good plans are frustrated; praiseworthy schemes issue in nothing; pious activities result in failure, because an inconstant will is allowed to bite them off.

Uncle John's tenacity was wonderful. It was hard to shake him off. We entered a house of our congregation with him one day where we met a young man from Virginia who had come North to attend school. The others present being Christians, Uncle John soon fastened all the conversation upon him. We never saw him so press and push a soul. He had found a lost sheep, and seemed determined, "shepherd's dog" that he was, to keep at it till he had worried it home. Again and again we feared that he was crowding too hard and too far. But he had been out on many such a service before, and what he was about he knew very well. Before the house was left, a sincere penitent was on his knees pleading for mercy, and was soon rejoicing in Christ as his portion. Three or four years have gone since then, and the one so wrestled with, a useful and earnest Christian now, has many a time blessed the Lord that he was not given up that day.

His *tact* was a characteristic that should not be underestimated or left unnamed.

"He seldom made a blunder. His knowledge of human nature seemed almost intuitive. He read men at a glance, and pierced the surface of things as by magic. He knew how to approach men, what to say to them, and when to have done with them. He adapted himself to all classes and conditions when talking of Christ. The school-girl or the college professor, the millionaire or the hard-handed son of toil, a sailor or a soldier—with equal readiness and skill he met them all. His mind was a perfect storehouse of

Scripture, and he had a verse on his tongue's end to serve him at every time." It must be a very dull man whom he could not make to see, a very hard man whom he could not make to feel, a very stubborn man whom he could not to some extent bend, and a very sharp one whom he could not match. When any one attempted to foil him he would head him off by a move that might be called a piece of strategy. "On one occasion" (this from Dr. G. M. Stone) "he went to visit a young lady for religious conversation. She saw him approaching, and went up stairs to avoid him. Uncle John, upon coming in, comprehended the situation at a glance, and requested that the door of the stairway might be opened. He then knelt at the foot of the stairs and sent up a melting petition to God in behalf of the person named."

He was equal to any emergency that might arise. If any imagined that, because his heart was so tender, he could be easily outgeneralled that, because he was guileless and unsuspecting, he could be taken at a disadvantage and put in an awkward place or plight, they would quickly find out their mistake. The *Christian Intelligencer* must be held responsible for this story —a story which illustrates this feature in his character, and is too good to be lost:

"While laboring in the Army of the Potomac he was called out of bed one night by a messenger, who represented that a soldier in a certain tent was in great distress of mind. On reaching the tent indicated he found several officers seated around a keg of beer which had been brought from Washington, and he was invited to join them and take a drink. Taking in the situation at a glance, he told them he could not do it without first asking the blessing of God. So, grasping the arm of the principal man, he fell on his knees and poured out an ardent prayer for the company, after which they were glad to let him go. The story got out, and for months afterward one of those men could hardly show his face without being asked about the prayer-meeting they had set up. Uncle John was too much for them."

Another who tells the story says that there were two prayers, and singing and exhortation beside.

Any number of illustrations might be given, as showing forth this characteristic, but we will add only this.

"Shortly after the evacuation of Richmond the American Tract Society sent a District Secretary with Uncle John into that city to establish a depository of its publications and a centre of colportage. As was right these brethren sought the cooperation, at least the approval, of the pastors of the churches, a company of whom had assembled to consider their duty in the new emergency. The Secretary being allowed to speak, expressed the wish of his Society to cooperate with the brethren in rebuilding the wastes of the war, in reorganizing their Sabbath-schools and granting them libraries in lieu of those scattered. A prominent and honored divine, still smarting under the inflictions of the Union army, repelled the proffered help, rejected the extended hand of Christian friendship, and said somewhat warmly his people would prefer publications with the imprint of London to that of New York. Others spoke, and a storm was evidently rising when Uncle John in his quick and gentle way said, 'Let us pray,' and without a moment's hesitation was upon his knees, and poured out such a prayer as melted and harmonized all hearts, and as they rose the venerable pastor with tears and a warm handshake, said, 'Brethren, I cannot stand any longer in opposition to your Christian offer. My heart is with you.' Soon thereafter a colporteur was appointed in his locality, and has ever since continued his labors in that and adjoining places."

This other trait was most remarkably manifest in the man: *Under all inequalities of circumstance or condition he saw a soul to be saved, and realized its worth.* When he went to call on the President of the United States he paid him the respect due to his high office, but did not let go of his hand till he had spoken to him of the Lord Jesus and put to him most courteously the question that was ever on his lips.

When he was introduced to Brigham Young in his Salt Lake City home he made the same appeal, and pressed the same searching inquiry on his soul. A distinguished Liberal Religionist of our day has tauntingly said that "evangelicals" had shown a remarkable indifference about his "salvation." Once only had anybody ever exhorted him to repentance, and then he himself drew the exhortation out. He never could have met John Vassar and afterward have truthfully said that.

But Uncle John was just as solicitous for a private in the army, a negro in his cabin, a child in the Sunday-school. There was no difference between them in his eyes.

This is the story which his friend Rev. Mr. Hazard tells: "Uncle John and myself occupied adjoining rooms in a boarding-house near the Capitol at Washington in the winter of 1867. On going down stairs to breakfast one morning I found him standing there in earnest conversation with one of the colored servants, and it needed but a hasty glance to see that he was urging a most tender and affecting appeal for immediate attention to the concerns of the soul. Class or color was of little consequence to him. He was a 'winner of souls,' and I doubt if he left one his equal in this land when he passed away."

He was a man of deep and tender *sympathy*.

No matter what indifference, ingratitude, or even imposition he encountered, nothing could freeze over, nay, even chill, the generous sensibilities of his soul. Suffering of any sort would touch him to the quick. Nor would he show it only by words and tears. A sympathy that had nothing but sentiment in it he rated cheap. He was emotional, but he was practical as well. Pity did not glisten in his eye and drop from his tongue only. It sent his feet running on errands, and his hand helping wherever there was need. When Dr. Tyng had him at the Gospel Tent work in New York City he carried not only the Bread of Life to starving souls, but many a literal loaf to hungry mouths.

Having access to our lines in war time to an extent which few enjoyed, he would fairly load himself down as he returned from Washington or Alexandria with parcels for the men. More than once he went from "the front" to the national capital when they were fifty miles apart to get some delicacies for suffering men, walking both ways, nor counted it a hardship as he trudged along.

In a time of affliction his heart went right out toward the smitten and sorrowing. He had gone through sore straits of anguish himself, and when others were in them he went to their sides to weep with those that wept and whisper of the Comforter.

While the body of Dr. Babcock lay in the house awaiting burial, Uncle John called, and was taken by the family into the room where the dear old pastor rested as if asleep. Approaching the casket, and looking down upon the face which death had so little changed, he exclaimed, "My Father, my Father, the chariot of Israel and the horsemen thereof." Then recalling the time of his conversion and the guiding counsels given by these now still lips, he said, "Under God I owe all that I am to this man." The prayer that followed we can imagine, not describe. The household group, bowed with him, say that while it was being offered they had such glimpses of the coming glory as lifted them on eagle's wings, and brought the deep peace of paradise very near.

Many a reader of this book will remember some similar scene. When the shadow of bereavement hung heavily over the heart and home, when the coffin or the new grave seemed somehow to have come between their souls and heaven, he carried them up to his Lord so lovingly, and laid them so feelingly in the Everlasting Arms, that the sorrow was half lifted and the shadows more than half swept away.

He was a man of marked *humility.*

We are quite sure that no one ever heard him utter a boastful word. "Unto me, who am *less than the least of all saints,* is this grace given;" this was the spirit in which he lived his life and did his work. He never sought to put himself forward or take the lead. No chaplain, preacher, pastor whom he was aiding ever felt that Uncle John was seeking to take the command or put the properly commissioned leader back. He was particularly careful to magnify the office of the Christian minister. In the agencies for bringing a lost world back to God he always put the living preacher first. Nor did he parade his personal piety, nor trumpet his attainments in the Christian life. Judged by all the standards that we know any thing about, the mark he reached was very high; but no one would have learned that from his lips.

Dr. Stone says, "I once asked him what he thought of the doctrine of perfect sanctification in this life. His answer was, 'I do not doubt we may have high experiences of Christ's love, and great degrees of submission and joy, *but the difficulty is to keep there.*' Many times since I have felt the wisdom and spiritual insight of his words."

So anxious was he to avoid even the appearance of egotism that it was difficult to get him to speak of details and results of work which many, when he was talking publicly and privately, would have been pleased to hear.

And there was no affectation in this. There is an assumed humility which is more disgusting and unbearable than outspoken, arrogant conceit. Any thing but a sanctimonious, abject air put on for effect's sake; a depreciation of self for the purpose of getting higher compliments. You can laugh at overweening vanity; the other thing excites contempt and scorn. Men saw that Uncle John's humility was genuine. Sincerity shone out in every word. He had no selfish ends to accomplish. He had no ambitious projects to carry out. The test he had to stand was searching. When a man emerges from obscurity to be recognized as a positive force in the religious movements of his age, the retaining of an unmagnified self-estimate is difficult indeed. But here was a man who bore the test. Let others say what they might, he knew that he was just John Vassar, nothing more and nothing less. Self-seeking of every sort he scorned; nay, more, he abhorred it from his very heart. All who came in contact with him saw that he was not striving for honor or grasping for money; he had just one object, and that was to save their souls.

This enumeration of characteristics would be incomplete if we failed to mention *the broad and catholic spirit of the man.*

Denominationally he was a Baptist. The peculiar views and practices of that branch of the Saviour's church he intelligently and conscientiously held. In the proper place he would maintain and defend them. He refused, however, again and again, to leave the service of the Tract Society to engage in purely denominational work. He felt he could reach more men on its union basis than he could if laboring in the interests of a particular sect. And to turn men to righteousness was more important in his estimation than the gathering of them around this peculiar standard or that. He rendered a loyal allegiance to the ensign of his own particular corps, but the one flag on which the cross was blazoned he would lift over all. Around that first he would rally men, and then afterward have them go into such church relations as each might choose.

This being his great aim; he went among all churches holding an evangelical faith, little caring what the name might be. And we doubt whether the sharpest-eared or the keenest-eyed critic would have detected the slightest difference in the testimony which he bore. One message he everywhere voiced. One need he emphasized. One Helper he pointed out. And it might be added that the style of working and the results witnessed were everywhere much the same—the same in kind at least if not in measure. We have in this volume statements from representative men in the Methodist, Baptist, Presbyterian, Lutheran, Congregational, Episcopal, and Reformed churches, touching this man and his labors, and so much alike are the opinions which they pass, and the affection they express, that all of them might have been written by any single hand.

The strongest points in the man's character have now been sketched. It will seem like a poor, dull picture to those who knew the original when he was at his best. It may help, however, to show what made him such a power. Give to any man such qualifications in any such degree, and he will make himself felt. Nothing so gets hold upon the world, nothing so keeps hold, as an unselfish, consecrated life.

One who has furnished some of the incidents mentioned here in a private note says: "You and I, and all who knew the man, have before us an evidence of the truth of the Gospel and a proof of its power. Whatever else may be quibbled about or argued away, the power which kept that man going, doing, praying, that cannot be disposed of either by logic or a sneer."

Mrs. John H. Ketcham, who was familiar with his army work, as well as many other labors, writing from Washington and speaking for herself and the General, says:

"Wherever his name was known it was the synonym for godliness—that is, Christlikeness; and 'greater honor hath no man than this.'

"He will always live in the hearts of those who knew him, and who beheld in him one without guile or thought of self, who gave his life to men and to the Master.

"Our recollections of him are of the pleasantest,

18*

and we are glad that the loveliness of his character and
the grandeur of a life so full of toil and sacrifice are to
be set forth."

It is very evident that men of this stamp are the great
need in all our Christian work. The age is positive, active, driving, and its wickedness is of a similar type.
Men of God who are going to meet it must match it in
resoluteness and aggressiveness. The question once
asked by the Master must be the question of those
who follow in his train, "Wist ye not that I must be
about my Father's business?" The motto for the hour
is, "At it, and ever at it, till He comes." The prevalent
piety is not of such a tone. Most of it is of a lower grade.
It is decent, moderate, quiet. Spiritual indolence is in
these times the worst foe our holy religion has to encounter. It is not that men openly reject and make war
upon it, but that they drowsily sleep around its altars.
It is that they are content with such paltry satisfactions
and tinsel comforts as the senses can bribe them with,
heedless of what bids them claim communion with the
skies. It is that eternity has no awfulness to them, life no
depth of meaning, enjoyment no obligations, bereavement no solemnity, suffering and sorrow no prophetic
suggestions of an hereafter, conscience no echo of God,
Christ no enrapturing beauty, holiness no pledge of
heaven." Next to the Holy Spirit in its sevenfold energies
the great want of the church is godly men: men girded with awful zeal; men who beg no favors of worldly
policy; men who have the staunch, uncompromising

sincerity of old confessors, and yet whose speech is the benediction of charity. Men who will thrust in the unwilling face of darkness all the light of God, and whom no disappointments can palsy, no opposition embitter, and no misgivings keep back. Given such men, and they will have influence. Skeptics, moralists, easy-going religionists, will feel it. They may not understand it, they may not like it, but there will be something real about it; and, after all, reality is what this world wants. When it sees a man who acts as if this earth were a show and a dream, and his home over in "the blue eternities," somehow it will feel that he has something which it lacks. Uneasiness begins to stir. There is a disposition to say, "After all, this is what we want. We are not satisfied. We are not happy. We are not at peace. It's all a make-believe, a cheat, a lie. Tell us how we can be made better, holier; how we can front God, and look the splendors of His judgment in the face."

We have plenty of machinery for the doing of evangelistic work, but machinery will accomplish no more toward bringing in Christ's kingdom than draining sand-deserts would do toward making them fruitful. Men of the right stamp—this is the crying want. These multiplied, and the cause of the Master might speedily move on to those victories which in Scripture are prophesied and pledged.

CHAPTER X.

THE VETERAN DISABLED.

"He holds me when the billows smite,
    I shall not fall.
If sharp 'tis short, if long 'tis light;
    He tempers all."

JAMES HAMILTON says that old age is a sort of Terra del Fuego, a region where the weather never clears. Cloud and drizzle darken and dampen many of its days, and there is little reason to expect that it will be otherwise while life shall last.

Uncle John could hardly be called old when he began to break. Before he had seen sixty years infirmities were pressing heavily, and thereafter he saw few hours altogether free from pain. It is not strange that it was so. The only wonder is that his bodily vigor was retained unimpaired so long. Had he not come of sturdy stock he could not have borne the strain of the previous five-and-twenty years. His unflagging spirit constantly overlooked the body, or overestimated and overtaxed its powers. Nature will ultimately exact the penalty for such violation of her laws. No matter how good the object in the attainment of which strength is overtasked, the effect is not likely to be averted or escaped. God wrought no miracle to save his servant from the consequences of his exhausting and almost superhuman work.

For the last three or four years he was much of the time really unfit to keep about. Mind and body had been kept on the tightest stretch. They now needed rest. But rest was precisely that of which he would not hear. His soul was as alert and eager as in his prime. Flesh and blood must serve it still. The feet must not stop running if they were tired. Let him keep right on till he dropped in the harness. That was the way he wanted it arranged. His Lord did not so order it.

A year before he entered on the rest that remaineth, the physical system got so utterly out of order that it stopped short, unable longer to obey the still resolute spirit that sought to urge it on.

The last public work undertaken was at Minden, Montgomery County, N. Y., the following account of which is given by Rev. J. H. Weber:

"In the summer of 1877, while visiting Coxsackie on the Hudson, I heard much of the labors which Uncle John had performed there the previous winter. It immediately occurred to me that he was just the man I had been praying for and looking for to assist me in meetings on my own field.

"Arrangements were made with the Tract Society, and on the third of December a letter came telling me to meet him at Fort Plain. When the train arrived the first man to step off was Uncle John. On the way to my house I saw he was sick, and determined to make it as comfortable and easy as possible by providing a warm room to stop in by night, and a horse to carry him around by day. He wanted to start out that very afternoon, but I persuaded him to rest.

"The next day we started out from house to house, and a day or two later he said to me, "Brother Weber, we have not got hold of the right string yet; but keep on praying, and the Lord will show it to us yet, before long.' That day I had a call for a funeral service at Bethel, and when he heard of it he appeared to feel impressed that the Lord would open the way there, and that that would be the place to take hold. During the funeral I was convinced that the Spirit was working there beyond a doubt, and so appointed meetings for the following week. The first night Uncle John did not get there, as he had a meeting fixed for elsewhere; but when an invitation was given nine rose for prayer.

"The next night he arrived and appeared to be in his element at once. He prayed, he sang, he talked, and the whole congregation seemed melted into tears. In his visitations no shop or store or house was passed.

"In one yard he saw a man of more than seventy chopping wood. Uncle John stopped and began to question him about his hope. He frankly avowed that he was a spiritualist, that he did not believe the Bible, but added that he was willing Uncle John should do all the good to others that he could. A few more words of entreaty were pressed on him, and then we passed along, Uncle John praying that God would 'save that dear old man.' Today he is a consistent Christian, and a member of the Lutheran church.

"Into the stores and shops he would often run for a few minutes, and talk to those there found, and sometimes offer prayer. One man since his death has said to me, 'I don't believe that I should ever have been converted if he had not come into my shop and prayed for me and plead with me as he did.'

"Sometimes a group of thoughtless or reckless young men would come into the evening service, and by talking and laughing disturb the meeting. Soon as any thing of the kind was begun, Uncle John would quietly move that way, and getting into the knot would drop down and offer such a prayer as would shame them, and sometimes solemnize every soul.

"So for two weeks the work went on, till the last night came that he was to be with us. Such words of encouragement to the converts, such exhortations to the ungodly, it seems to me I never heard, nor do I expect ever to hear their like again. When the address was finished he fell upon his knees and offered the last prayer we were ever to listen to from his lips. When the service was over all crowded around him, anxious for one more grasp of his hand. To each there was a word of personal advice and a 'God bless you,' to which many a heart sent back a like response. "When we parted the next morning, he said, 'The Lord be with you, my dear brother, and with this people; and remember old Uncle John Vassar sometimes in your prayers.'"

When he reached his home, with the last days of 1877, the labors of love which for more than a quarter of a century he had pushed so unremittingly were substantially at an end. For more than six months he lay entirely prostrate, passing through frequent paroxysms of pain that were pitiful to behold, and that medical skill was powerless to prevent or greatly lighten. When midsummer came he began to rally, and for a time it seemed not impossible that he might yet do a little light work in the vineyard of the Lord. He was seen upon the streets once more, and filled occasionally his seat in the sanctuary on the Sabbath or in the social meetings of the week. His once quick step had grown slow, but his voice was clear, and something of the old smile again lit up his face. It was only the brief brightening of the lamp, however, preparatory to the going out.

CHAPTER XI.

HONORABLY DISCHARGED.

"His soul to Him who gave it rose;
God led it to its long repose,
    Its glorious rest.
And though the warrior's sun has set,
Its light shall linger round us yet,
    Bright, radiant, blest."

WHEN fruit is altogether ripe it drops readily from the bough. Till then it clings with a tenacious hold. Uncle John did not at once let go of life. In spite of sufferings that at times were terrible, he was in no hurry to shake off mortality and have the battle done. Not only was the life instinct strong, but he saw much yet remaining to be done, and in the doing of it he would fain bear a part.

In the early autumn of 1878 the tokens of improvement noticed in the previous chapter were quite marked. He regarded them as indications to buckle the harness on again, and began to lay plans for the weeks ahead.

Under date of October 1st, to Rev. Mr. Owen, of Wyoming County, N. Y., he thus writes:

"DEAR BROTHER OWEN: I am getting better every day, and can work some. Please write to New York to the Secretary, Rev. G. L. Shearer, and see if I can-

not come to you at once. I think the Lord will work for
His glory in your place. How can I reach you, and what
will be the railroad fare?"

October 9th he sends another postal, reading thus:

"The Society and my doctor both say I cannot come
to you; but I want to come and see the salvation of
our God once more. Send me a card and tell me the
route."

The Society now interposed its authority, and pe-
remptorily forbade him to engage in any kind of work.
They saw the ruling passion so asserting itself, and
were so fearful it might hurry him into engagements
that he was utterly unfit to fill that they even required
him for his own protection to sign a paper obligating
himself for the present to keep still. The enforced idle-
ness was painful to him, and but for the giving of such
a promise he would probably have made some feeble
and futile attempt to gird on the old responsibilities.

October came toward its close, and though weak he
was tolerably comfortable. With the last days of the
month the Prophetic Conference was to meet in the
church of his good friend, Dr. S. H. Tyng, Jr. He felt
sure he might venture to attend this gathering, and
the family, seeing his anxiety, assented to his plans.
Accompanied by his eldest son, he went to New York,
visited again those with whom he had been so long associated in the Tract House, and spent a pleasant Sabbath among dear Christian friends. The meetings of

the Conference in Holy Trinity, where he had enjoyed some blessed seasons previously, were to him a great delight. He was a firm believer in the general doctrines there discussed, and had been for many years. His saintly father had held to "that blessed hope," and to Uncle John it was just as sweet. Concerning it we are not here called upon to speak. Only this in passing should be said, that if the doctrine—as is sometimes urged—does relax the hand of pious effort, and weaken faith in the Gospel's power to save, it certainly did not produce in him its natural fruits.

This reunion with old brethren and friends seemed to act like a tonic. He was more like himself than he had been for months. Dr. Tyng says that as he went out from the church for the last time he looked up at it, and thinking of the great numbers who in it, or through its services, had been led to Christ, he lifted up his hands and said, *"God bless the dear old soul-trap."*

Inelegant the term, but blessedly expressive.

For a week or more after reaching home he seemed better than before his trip. He was able to attend one or two of the evening meetings in his own church, and those who listened to him said that almost the old fire and fervor appeared to flash. Then came a most distressing relapse. All the favorable symptoms disappeared. The two elder boys–one from New York, and one from St. Louis–were summoned home.

Three weeks of intense suffering followed, completely exhausting his little remaining strength. There were no spiritual raptures such as many supposed would be given him on a dying bed. As the body wasted, the quick, active mind declined. The strong, earnest spirit seemed to share in the prostration of the earthly house it so long had lived in. The mortal tabernacle was falling, and the immortal tenant felt the jar.

We might have wished it otherwise, but the Lord makes no mistakes. It is best to say about it or look at it as Paul did when he said, "The good and acceptable and perfect will of God." Even had he been granted the most triumphant death-bed, that could have added little to the testimony which had for thirty years been borne.

The last day came. It was Friday, December 6th. His faithful medical attendant, Dr. A. B. Harvey, came in to make his usual call. For more than a quarter of a century he had been the family physician, the firm friend, the loving Christian brother. His practised eye saw that the end was not far away, and a few hours later he came again. Then frankly he told the sinking man that the parting time had come. Tenderly he recalled their past experiences, joyfully he spoke of their common hopes, tearfully he bade him good-by till they should meet again in the house of many mansions. The departing veteran seemed surprised. He had not thought the change so near. Even when so plainly told that he was at the river's brink and soon must go across, only partially did he appear to realize the fact, and parted with the doctor as if fully expecting to see him the following day.

In the afternoon the household became convinced that only a few hours remained. All gathered around his bed—the wife, who for twenty-four years had been his companion and counsellor, Walter, Albert, Hattie, Johnnie—the living children of his love. He knew them all, and seemed pleased that they were near. That was about all he appeared to note. The brief December day darkened into night. The group of watchers was enlarged by the arrival of a sister, a niece, and one or two other friends. Gently, painlessly, but silently, he was passing into the presence of the holy God. An hour before the end came the lips moved, and the wife, bending over him, caught the word " farewell—farewell." Once again there was a faint whisper. It was "Hallelujah!" just that, and nothing more.

A little after seven o'clock the last breath fluttered from between the whitening lips. The soldier had received his discharge. The victor had gone to get and wear his crown.

> "One day, his voice was heard in Israel
> Amid her bannered legions, crying Cheer!
> To God's elected hosts in holy war;
> Another, and he dropped his tempered blade,
> And hushed his battle-cry, his warning note,
> And trailed his standard in the dust of death.
> But 'twas a glorious exchange for him!
>
> His sword laid down, he took the sceptre up;
> His call to arms, changed to the victor's song;
> His war-worn banner, to triumphant robes;
> His dying bed, to an undying throne."

The roof which sheltered his dying head was the

19*

gift of some loving Christian friends. He left nothing besides to the widow and the children, save a spotless name, and a record of heroic devotion and saintly sacrifice which this generation has yet to see surpassed.

On Monday afternoon, December 9th, those who loved the man bore his body to its rest. The day was dark with storm. Early there was a heavy snow-fall, later came on a drenching rain. The church on Mill Street nevertheless was filled. Taking into account the condition of the streets, it was as large a funeral gathering as Poughkeepsie has often seen. The city of his birth and lifelong residence kept a sacred memorial day. Uncle John's favorite Psalm, the one hundred and third, was read by his long-time friend, Dr. Stone, of Tarrytown.

Dr. Kendrick, his pastor, then dwelt briefly on the man's career. "If I were preaching a funeral sermon over Uncle John," he said, "this should be my text: 'The zeal of thine house hath eaten me up.'

"If he had a coat of arms, the proper device for it would have been a burning heart. Though zealous, he was not censorious. He lived in a higher sphere of spiritual life than his brethren, but he was always most patient with them. 'He allured to heaven and led the way.' Though his zeal was not properly one-sided or narrow, it still took very much the direction of anxiety for souls. And his efforts always kept even pace with his intense desires. If no opportunities offered for doing good, he went in search of them. In this respect I have never known his like."

Dr. Stephen H. Tyng, Jr., of New York, followed Dr. Kendrick. He said: "I parted with Uncle John at the throne of grace; I expect to meet him next at the throne of glory. He was like Bunyan in the originality and depth of his experience; like Harlan Page in his personal endeavors; like Hedley Vicars in his soldierly firmness. He might have been a capitalist, but he chose to live for Christ. His history will stand out as a representation of all unselfishness."

Rev. Dr. Fulton, of Brooklyn, said: "In this life now closed I hear the echoes of that apostolic shout of triumph, 'Thanks be unto God who always causeth us to triumph in Christ.' Uncle John took no glory to himself; he found in the Lord Jesus the source of his power, and the earnest of his victory. He started as a humble colporteur. He grew to be a master in Israel. It was in Boston I first saw him. There was a meeting in Tremont Temple, and God was there. Uncle John was in the city, and having a spare hour, dropped in. I obtained his help for a while. How he took hold! I hardly saw him, but how he did pull sinners out of the fire! Day after day he brought in trophies and laid them at the Master's feet. Once I got him on a Sunday afternoon to take my place in the pulpit at the 'Temple' and address the crowds that filled those seats. It was one of the most impressive discourses I ever heard.

"In the school-houses and country churches of

New England his face has been seen. Over its bleak hills and through its valleys his feet have carried him as he sought the wandering sheep. He is now with Jesus, and is crowned a hero evermore."

Rev. Dr. Stevenson and Rev. George L. Shearer, Secretaries of the Tract Society, were on the platform, and the former spoke of the traits of character which made Uncle John "the most laborious and the most useful Christian layman of his age." He was declared to have been "undisguisedly frank and straightforward, fearless in reproof, unflinching in maintaining the right, gently firm in reclaiming the erring, magnetic in action, fervent in prayer, convincing in argument, resistless in appeal, wise in all necessary worldly wisdom, undisturbed in emergencies, and, above all and beyond all, had all these characteristics so suffused and energized and directed by the Spirit of Christ as to make him the most successful lay missionary of modern days."

Rev. J. Hyatt Smith uttered the closing words. He said: "John Vassar illustrated more fully than any man whom I ever knew the apostle's ideal," diligent in business, fervent in spirit, serving the Lord.' " Tenderly and touchingly he dwelt upon the intimacies and memories of thirty years, and the ties which during those years had not only been preserved unweakened, but had steadily grown stronger.

Dr. Wheeler, of Poughkeepsie, pastor of the Presbyterian Church, then led in prayer, thanking God for the man, and the grace that had made him what he was; and then the choir, as a fitting close to what had been a joyful and triumphant service, sang:

> "I know not the hour when my Lord shall come
> To take me away to His own dear home;
> But I know that His presence will lighten the gloom,
> And that will be glory for me."

After the singing, hundreds passed around to look upon the well-known face— "a face that, despite the storm, despite suffering, despite death, was in perfect peace."

It was a mixed company that passed by the casket for a parting look. The most honored citizens of the community were in it, and every intermediate social grade between them and the poorest blacks, and by all he was sincerely mourned.

The afternoon was far spent when his beloved brethren, Richard Brittain, Thomas Hull, Stephen Hull, R. E. Lansing, Christian Mattern, James Smiley, and Adam Caire, as bearers, laid the body in the receiving tomb on the Hudson's banks, resting in the blessed trust expressed in Christian prayer for ages, that "through the grave and gate of death" he should "pass to a joyful resurrection."

Another has sweetly voiced the feelings with which we left the worn-out tabernacle for a little season there.

> From north and south, from east and west,
> Bring flowers, a wreath to twine
> Above the soldier laid to rest,
> This friend of thine and mine.

O'er hill and vale, with tireless feet,
  Glad messages he bore–
The story of the cross so sweet:
  He told it o'er and o'er.

That voice is hushed in silence now,
  The folded hands at rest;
Soft pillowed is the weary brow,
  In dreamless slumber blest.

Then twine a wreath of sweetest flowers
  And place it o'er his brow:
The sadness and the grief are ours:
  He's "more than conqueror" now.

M. H. W.

SOUTHFIELD, MASS., DEC. 17, 1878

CHAPTER XII.

SERVICE REVIEWED.

"Champion of Jesus—man of God,
Servant of Christ, well done!
Thy path of thorns hath now been trod,
Thy red-cross crown is won."

THE natural limits of this memoir have been already reached. The story of this humble, godly, useful life has been told, and it might properly be left to go before men's eyes without the addition of another line.

But in Dr. Tyng's and Rev. Mr. Brouner's churches in New York, in Dr. Fulton's and J. Hyatt Smith's in Brooklyn, in Rev. Mr. Twichell's in Hartford, Conn., in Rev. Mr. Holman's, Bunker Hill, Boston, and elsewhere, memorial sermons were preached, or memorial services held, the Sabbath following the burial of Uncle John; and these unusual, perhaps unprecedented, marks of affection and respect demand some recognition here.

Articles, moreover, from at least fifty different papers, secular and religious, are in our hands, all paying tributes to the man such as fall to the lot of few.

The material thus furnished has been largely drawn on in the preparation of this book. The commemorative meetings in the Holy Trinity and North Churches, of

New York, however, have not been referred to in these pages, and several newspaper articles, graphic and beautiful, have been left unused, because of an unwillingness to insert them in fragments or parts.

To these tributes let us devote a few leaves.

Of the gathering in Dr. Tyng's church on Sunday evening, December 15th, we have only the meagre press report. The night was unpropitious, but the attendance was very Large.

"The pastor in opening the service said that he had thought of draping the pulpit in mourning, but on reconsideration he concluded that it would be out of harmony with the cheerful spirit of him who had just entered into his rest. He would therefore ask the congregation, instead of lamenting, to unite in singing a hymn of triumph– 'Whom have I in heaven but Thee.'

"The singing over, Dr. Tyng remarked that Robert Hall, in conversation with Wilberforce, said that his idea of heaven was that it was a place of rest. Wilberforce replied that his idea was that it was all love. In the faith of John Vassar the ideas of rest and love were about equally blended.

"The Rev. G. L. Shearer, of the Tract Society, speaking of his army labors, said that he seemed to be everywhere where he was most wanted. He marched with the soldiers and bore all their hardships, carrying often the guns and knapsacks of younger men whose strength had failed. In the hospital he was as tender as a mother to the wounded men. When too weak to feed themselves, he would feed them, and sometimes take a spade and dig their graves. His labors among the miners of the West, the Mormons, and the freedmen, were also illustrated and described.

"General Clinton B. Fisk said: In camp and march and bivouac, in field and fight and hospital, Uncle John was a true soldier of the cross. He was a Moody and Sankey combined. His sweet voice could be heard at all times sounding the praises of Jesus. When, after hard days in the field, the officers would say, 'Uncle John, you're tired,' his cheery voice would reply in song:

'One more day's work for Jesus!
How sweet the work has been!'

Dr. J. D. Fulton said: 'Uncle John Vassar is to me the marvel of the age. I know of at least three services in memory of the man which are this hour being held, and tears are falling over his departure in the pine woods of Maine, among the mines and mountains of California, and the cotton fields and savannas of the South. He was a wonderful illustration of religion, pure and undefiled. It is with unfeigned gratitude to God that this statement can be made in this and any other presence, and have it stand unchallenged as an admitted truth.' The reverend doctor briefly referred to the talking gifts of the old veteran, and concluded by saying that America would yet venerate his name as England venerates the name of Bunyan.

"At the North Baptist Church the pastor, Rev. J.

20

J. Brouner, and Dr. A. S. Patton, gave many facts to illustrate his deep humility and thorough consecration. Among the reminiscences of his pious and unaffected ingenuity in commending Christ to men, Dr. Patton referred to having introduced him to the proprietor of a noted summer resort who was a pronounced Unitarian. Uncle John broke forth into a strain of eloquent admiration of the beauty of the surrounding scenery, made all the more charming to him because displaying the wisdom and power and goodness of his heavenly Father. 'But,' said he, 'His great love, manifested in giving His dear Son to die for sinners, eclipses everything else.' And then, with tremulous voice and tearful eye, he added, 'How the dear Lord Jesus did love us!"

Of the newspaper articles we select seven or eight from representative men in various branches of Christ's church.

The first is from the pen of Rev. A. J. Gordon, D. D., in the *Watchword.*

"The record of John E. Vassar's death will awaken little comment, perhaps, in the world; but I venture to say that it marks a welcome into the presence of Christ in Paradise such as few saints have received in modern times. I am sure that hundreds will concur with me in the opinion that since the days of Harlan Page the world has had few, if any, such workers for Christ as this dear man of God. His zeal and consecration were so intense, indeed, that it astonished moderate Christians, and often compelled him to hear even from the lips of Christ's professed disciples the charge, 'Thou art beside thyself.' But often as he met that reproof it never offended him. His reply was ever that of the great apostle: 'For whether we be beside ourselves, it is to God; or whether we be sober, it is for your cause. For the love of Christ constraineth us.' Those of us who knew him intimately know how blessedly sane he was on all high themes of divine love and holy obedience to Christ Jesus the Saviour; how rational he was when judged by the text, 'For me to live is Christ.' He was eccentric only as the orbit of the sun is eccentric to that of a wandering star. He kept the orbit in which Christ his Master had put him so steadily and so unswervingly that easy-going, half-hearted Christians were amazed and perplexed. Indeed, far beyond any man whom I ever knew, was it true of him that his citizenship was in heaven; and so filled was he with the glory and the power of the heavenly life, that to many he seemed like a foreigner speaking an unknown language.

But how good it was to be with him, and to be kindled by the intense ardor of his consecration!

"I gladly and gratefully pay this tribute to his memory, that I have never been so humbled and quickened by contact with any living man as with him.

"He was not a preacher, but counted it his special calling to go from house to house, beseeching men, in Christ's stead, to be reconciled to God. Often he would so impress ministers, who heard him talk, with his intense

and burning earnestness, that they would urge him
to preach for them; but his pleasant reply always was,
'Oh, no! I am not a pastor, but only a shepherd's dog,
ready to run after the lost sheep, and try to bring them
home to the Shepherd.' And that work he pursued with
marvellous consecration and singleness of purpose.

"If he found himself obliged to wait a few minutes
for dinner, he would often say, 'Yes; and, while you are
getting ready, let me step out and see such and such a
one. I think the Spirit of God is working on his heart.'
He took almost no time for rest. He did not walk about
his Master's business; he literally ran. "The King's
business requireth haste,' was his motto. Bright will
be his crown. Multitudes will rise up at the last day
and call him blessed. He journeyed through all parts
of our great country, never halting, never tiring, bent
only on fulfilling the mission to which God had called
him. Four or five successive seasons he labored with
me in the gospel. When he came he always took the
church at once upon his heart, and literally travailed
in prayer for the unconverted among us. The nights
which he spent at my house were nights of prayer and
pleading for my congregation and my ministry.

"If any one would like to know whether there is anything practical in living in the power of 'that blessed
hope,' looking daily for the return of the Lord Jesus
from heaven, let this life answer. The imminence of
Christ's coming, the possibility of living to see the
Lord appearing in glory, was with him a daily inspiration and a most powerful motive. Often have

I heard him speak of this theme, and express the longing that all Christians might 'love His appearing.' From waiting on earth, he has gone to wait in Paradise.

"Farewell, dear man of God. Hundreds of Christians, while sorrowing that they shall see thy face no more for the present, will bless God, as long as they live, for the quickening and inspiration which they received from thy devoted life."

Rev. John W. Harding, in the Congregationalist, contributes this equally appreciative sketch:

"Multitudes who have been greatly indebted for spiritual help to this beloved disciple tenderly lament his departure, and rejoice in his glorious welcome to the nearer presence of his Lord. Soldiers who wore the blue and gray; Christian- and Sanitary-Commission men and women; many repenting sinners and returning backsliders; others to whom he has been a son of consolation in their poverty and affliction; many wavering ones whom he has brought to decision; many pastors whom he has edified and instructed in needed points of spiritual experience and pastoral deficiency—rise up now, with swift accord, to call him blessed.

"What a good fight was his! Despised, rebuffed, persecuted, he held right on, meekly and joyfully, in his simple, earnest, faithful way, his little worn Testament in hand, his single eye fixed on Jesus, Master, Saviour of lost souls; his lips moving, even when no voice was heard, in unceasing prayer; ready to break forth in some familiar song; his spiritual intuitions,

20*

quick to discern the real soul-needs of others, and just so quick to impart in searching, yet loving, words the remedy.

"Uncle John, while most persistent in seeking after souls, was at the same time the humblest of men. He esteemed ministers very highly in love, for their work's sake. It has rejoiced many a pastor's heart to know how he was praying, and getting others to pray, for the success of the next sermon, and to look from the pulpit into his earnest, tearful, observant eye, taking in every word with such appreciative interest, glancing over the congregation to measure if he could the effect of the discourse, his prayers meanwhile going up unceasingly for particular souls.

"Rebuffs, coldness, insults, were nothing, save that they made him sad for others' sake. He passed on to another house, and soon forgot the momentary sting or smart. No harshness could quench the ardor of his affection. No one had any need to ask his forgiveness. It had already beamed in joy over the returning sinner, not for his own, but for Jesus' sake.

"It was my inestimable privilege in the earlier part of my ministry to sit at the feet of Uncle John as he taught more effective methods of pastoral work in the care of souls. I met him for the first time at the railroad station one lovely day in April, he having come to spend a week with me in pastoral visitation. While the hands were yet grasped there was established a bond of sympathy. There was no time, he thought, to lose. We must begin our work right there. The family of the depot master was nearest, and before ten minutes had passed one lonely and discouraged soul, a wanderer from the fold, was giving out with quivering lip and moistened eyes her heart's secret and confiding depths, and we had knelt together at the heavenly throne. And so we went from house to house as they came in order, my heart fuller and fuller of sweet surprises at the swift access which the stranger friend acquired as by some talismanic power.

"It was the power of the Holy Ghost that was in him, and which he seemed to impart to me as by a magnetic sympathy.

"It was again the power of a large spiritual experience of his own, enriched by extensive insight and observation. His intuitions were quick, his questions intelligent and direct, his diagnosis accurate. Not a moment's time did he waste in beating the bush, in making careful and roundabout approaches. The simple preparatory question was: 'My dear friend, have you experienced that change of heart that the Saviour calls being born again?' The gentle frankness of the question usually elicited a frank reply. If there was hesitation through spiritual doubt and darkness, Uncle John was quick, in manifest sympathy, to draw out the real soul conditions, and their causes in the past. There was no delusive consolation, no smoothing over the case with 'uncertain remedies, or the offering of delay. Now must be the accepted time, and the decisive moment, and the case must be laid directly before the waiting Lord in prayer. No unnecessary time must be spent in urging duty when the light had come. There were other souls who demanded us, and we moved on.

"What revelations by the way, some cheering and others sad, but when day was over and the night far spent, what thrilling and abundant occasions for prayer that was prayer, at our family altar. And what occasions for preaching, too; different preaching, thoughtful, well-aimed, the winged arrows, the sword of the Spirit drawn from its scabbard, the encouragements and helps that must be given.

"No professorship of pastoral care has ever taught our theological students what John Vassar would have taught them in one day's experience from house to house. How sad the ignorance with which our youthful ministers often go out from their long years of scholastic training into the common life of the people whose souls are committed to their charge!

"What a glorious power would our Christianity put on if in every church there should be even one man or woman with the spiritual energy, and motive and tact to use it that Uncle John possessed!"

Rev. Theodore L. Cuyler, D. D., gives us this, in the *Evangelist*:

"Uncle John Vassar was one of the remarkable characters who came to the front during the civil war. With its religious history his name is as indelibly linked as the names of Chaplain McCabe, or D. L. Moody, or George H. Stuart. Hundreds of soldiers, when they read the tidings of his death, will recall the beloved old man, in his brown coat and soft felt hat, who used to tramp from tent to tent with a satchel of Bibles and tracts on his back. Nor did he only carry good books in that well-known satchel. He always had a supply of envelopes and postage stamps, and a needle and thread to mend a ragged uniform, or some knick-knack which soldiers always need.

"One thing he was sure to have, and that was a word in season. A negro in the army gave a capital description of the veteran colporteur when he said, 'I just tell you what I think of Uncle John; he is a *real Christianity.*'

"And so he was. You could not meet John Vassar on a steamboat, or in a street car, or anywhere without being kindled by his fresh, earnest talk. Even as Jacob brought the smell of the barley-field and the vineyard in his garments, so this good old man carried the flavor of his religion with him wherever he went.

"Sometimes during his visits to Brooklyn he used to drop into our church prayer-meeting and modestly take his seat by the door. We were always sure to hear from him, and his words were nails in a sure place. He always illustrated what power there is in Christian laymen when they will 'witness' freely and on all fit occasions for their divine Master. Today this land needs a hundred thousand Vassars to supplement the work of the pulpit and the Sabbath-school.

"Dear old Uncle John has reached his last bivouac. The tireless frame that scoured the prairies of Illinois, and the camps of the Union armies, and the rural regions of North Carolina and Virginia, and the everglades of Florida, is smoothed to its last quiet sleep.

The soldiers and the negro freedmen will bless his memory. And many a polished pastor and profound scholar may at the last great day envy the crown and the reward of that sturdy minister in homespun—brave John Vassar."

Rev. Charles S. Hageman, D.D., of Nyack, N. Y., but long pastor of the Second Reformed Church, Poughkeepsie, has this to say:

"John Vassar was known to me personally for at least twenty-five years. I have been with him often and much in Christian work. We have labored together in revival work, and talked and planned for the extension of that work. He was always the same— 'a man full of faith and of the Holy Ghost,' never despondent, always hopeful.

"One thing seemed to occupy his thoughts and to engross his life, and that one thing was the salvation of sinners and the glory of God. You could not meet him even on the street for five minutes without seeing what was the great absorbing interest of his soul.

"He was very *careful* and *prudent* in what he did. He had great respect for the ministry, and always sought on entering a place to secure first of all their counsel and co-operation. 'Brother Hageman,' he would say, 'the ministry is God's appointment for saving men, and nothing can take its place. Whatever other evangelistic agencies may be employed, the preached Word is and will remain the great power unto salvation.' He frequently came into my study to talk with me about the Lord's work, and always before parting he would propose a season of prayer. I was always glad to join in it, his heart was so mellow with love to Christ and for souls, and he so wrestled at the mercy-seat in my behalf.

"All the glory of everything accomplished he gave to God. I never heard a word from his lips that could be interpreted to mean the glorifying of himself. Self was lost in love for Christ.

"In parting from him I cannot but say, 'Well done, good and faithful servant.' May the mantle of the father fall upon the children. May I not add, upon the ministry of Christ ?"

> "O man of wondrous piety,
> And marked by such humility;
> Who waits thy mantle to receive,
> Like thee to love, as thee believe?
> The meek disciple everywhere,
> No sham, pretence, but steeped in prayer."

Another adds: "How much Christ was to him! His heart was aglow with the sense of what he had done, and was doing, and was going to do for him. How sweetly and eloquently he would dwell upon the scenes of our Saviour's life! They seemed to be always before him. His soul feasted upon them. They came into his dreams. The memory of Christ was the conscious fountain of his motive.

"He was so humble, so brotherly, so loyal, so true. A right noble helper he proved to be, interesting himself as much as if it were his own parish, but always and scrupulously keeping himself in the shadow as it were of the pastor. He positively would not take the lead where the pastor was present. Efficient as he was, wise as he was, able as he was to exhort, it must always be as second to the pastor, and his helper. In this, he was an evangelist of the old school, to which Dr. Nettleton and Dr. Kirk belonged. His coming and his going were both calculated to strengthen the pastor's hands and to tighten his hold in the parish.

"There was nothing of professionalism in his way of doing things and with tact and knowledge of human nature equal to his zeal, he was enabled to turn defeat into success. Such a life shows that the religion of Christ is still what it was in the days of the apostles."

Rev. Stephen H. Tyng, Jr., D. D., rector of the Church of the Holy Trinity, New York, and one of Uncle John's warmest friends, adds the following testimony:

"THE GOSPEL TENT, NEW YORK CITY.

"UNCLE JOHN VASSAR IN THE GOSPEL TENT! WHO CAN DEscribe him? Who among us was able to comprehend him? What memories of his fidelity and tenderness still abide among us! Wonderful old man! 'When shall we see thy like again?' His was an almost inconceivable zeal, an unflagging energy, and these were connected with a temper as tender as that of a child.

"This special work to which I am about to allude was really begun in the fall of 1875, as an effort preparatory to the Hippodrome services of Messrs. Moody and Sankey. But it long survived its occasion. At the close of the Moody meetings the same kind of labor was employed in the Church of the Holy Trinity, and Uncle John was our leader. But as summer approached we purchased and pitched the Gospel Tent. It was circular in form, one hundred feet in diameter, and forty-five feet high at the central pole. It had a seating capacity of two thousand persons, though by the use of the "much grass" in the adjoining lots, additional hundreds were often brought under the influence of the Gospel as preached from its platform. During four months our friend and brother continued his ministry in connection with this tabernacle. Its seals remain with us to this day. Scores were by him led to the Lord, and hundreds were helped and comforted by his apt words of encouragement and consolation.

"I shall never forget the early morning prayer-meeting on June 11th, 1876, when we dedicated the tent to the worship of Jesus. The day was bright and cool. There was a benediction in the breath of the morning air. Uncle John seemed to perceive it. When I asked him to make the prayer of dedication—before we ran the flag bearing the words 'The Gospel Tent' to the perch of the central pole—his heart was greatly enlarged. I have no doubt that he had spent a large portion of the previous night in intercession for the work. His words were mighty as he implored a Divine blessing. But when his voice was toned to thanksgiving, it seemed to us as though we should lose him in a rapture. With wonder we were led with Elisha to say, 'O my father! my father!'

"At every succeeding daily service, noon and

21

night, he was always on the platform and in the inquiry room. His keen eye watched the congregation during preaching, and immediately at its close he was by the side of some anxious soul whose interest he had through spiritual discernment detected. And how gentle was he with such! No shepherd ever carried lambs more tenderly in his arms. During the daytime he spent the hours in visitation. The thermometer marked 90° very often, but he was undaunted. His physical disorders might well have excused him, but the spirit compelled the flesh to "go about doing good.' The success of this tent work, under God, was largely due to his untiring labor.

"The quaint things which he said and did have their place among our *memorabilia.* I remember his criticism upon a very devout woman who had aided us greatly in the work of the tent. The epithet is always suggested by a sight of her face. "Beloved,' he said, 'that good woman is a *chunk of rock salt.*' On the only occasion when an Episcopal minister of High Church tendencies preached in the tent, Uncle John was very much excited. He rejoiced in spirit that Christ was preached in any way. A true Pauline joy he had. His ejaculations through the sermon somewhat disturbed the preacher, but the good man could not repress them. And when the sermon was concluded, Uncle John prayed—and such a prayer! It gathered up every possible want, and especially wrestled for a blessing upon the preacher, who was greatly overcome by its sincerity and intensity. But it was such a shock to the preacher's churchly prejudices that he disappeared as soon as the prayer was concluded. To the day of his death Uncle John had no truer admirer than that man.

"This sketch of a noble and self-sacrificing work is most unsatisfactory to me, but the space at my disposal permits nothing more. Heaven is to me more real since this good man has gone. He lived in heaven even while he walked on earth. The savor of his holy life among us is a most sweet and sanctifying memory. 'May God grant us grace to live and labor like him, and then join him in his well-earned rest.'"

From Rev. Charles H. Spurgeon's *Sword and Trowel,* London, England.

"Uncle John not only deserves to be called a 'good soldier:' he was something more, for, while fighting the Lord's battles himself, he was an active recruiting sergeant, and never seems to have missed a chance of pressing home the question, 'Who is on the Lord's side?' To be 'instant in season' is a lower grade of Christian service; to be 'instant out of season' is the higher form of Christian consecration. Uncle John's labors were always in season, for he adapted himself to the sphere in which he was placed, and so compelled his opportunities that they were 'unseasonably in season.' He was one of the few men who approached Edward Irving's idea of an apostolic missionary, a man of one thought, the Gospel of Christ—of one purpose, the glory of God. Sublimely imprudent, as the world counts wisdom, he was wise in winning souls. His methods were unique, and his tact was inspired by the singleness of his aim and the wisdom and energy by which he sought its realization. Whole-hearted in his consecration, he was untiring in his labors, and not only seized existing opportunities for usefulness, but created them.

"Resisted or repulsed in his spiritual warfare, he never was vanquished. The word defeat was not to be found in his vocabulary, for in all his encounters if one weapon failed him he was at no loss to command another. He courted the hand-to-hand encounter like the warriors of olden days, and wandered like a knight-errant in quest of the 'king's enemies,' whom he sought to conquer and enlist. It is impossible to contemplate his triumphs without feeling a thrill of admiration for the man, and the quickening of the desire, if not the determination, to emulate the example of his life. Cast upon the resources of his own energy in early life he acquired the habit of self-reliance, and learned to succeed where others would have failed. When recruiting for the service of the Lord this habit became an important factor. He could dare and do alone what others would hesitate to attempt. Dauntless courage and persistent energy, when sanctified by divine grace, make up the heroism of martyrs. Nothing but a seven days' religion suited Uncle John. To him it was marvellous that Christians were not all alive, and always alive to the work of soul-winning. No sooner was he converted than he commenced a career of usefulness in which the ardor of enthusiasm seemed to intensify with his years. Loyal to Christ he was always eager to lay some trophy at the Saviour's feet. 'He counted not his life dear unto him' in his passionate yearning to save souls. 'All the world was his parish,' 'every creature' the object of his solicitude. From the altitude to which he was raised by his divine commission, 'social distinctions were dwarfed, and all the diversities of nationality and class were merged in the common condition of universal ruin. To him the inspired verdict, 'There is no difference, for all have sinned,' established an equality of need; while the comprehensive assertion, There is no difference, for the same Lord over all is rich unto all that call upon him,' armed him with authority to carry the gospel to every member of the brotherhood of man.

"In every special mission he undertook, Uncle John more than justified the designation by which he was known, 'The Shepherd's Dog.' There was a reflex influence attending his labors. If, as the shepherd's dog, he went forth and brought home the wandering sheep, the pastors were stirred up to care for them in the fold. If he endeavored to raise the churches to a higher spirituality, he left them with a quickened desire, and the fixed resolution to copy an example so Christ-like. While his strength continued Uncle John held on, and when his health failed he was impatient of the restraint which loving friends imposed when it was clear to them he had 'fought the good fight.' Like a Chelsea pensioner the veteran, in recounting his victories, would not admit his incapacity for active service. Dear old man! the ruling passion was strong in death. As he had spent himself in the service of the Lord, there was a solemn fitness in the last words which fell from his lips, 'Farewell!' 'Hallelujah,' and 'when he had said this he fell asleep.' "

21*

"With loving heart and tearful eye,
Sad friends were gathered near,
To watch the Christian hero die
A death disarmed of fear.

" 'Farewell! Farewell!' he murmured low,
Then o'er those death-dimmed eyes
One glimpse of glory seemed to glow,
And Hallelujahs rise.

"O'er hill and vale the breezes swell,
A requiem soft and sweet,
Farewell! a tender last Farewell!
Till we in heaven shall meet."

The following is by Rev. Gideon Draper, in the *Christian Advocate.*

"It has passed into a truism, that religious zeal is a condition of religious success. And yet it is a truism that ever needs fresh enforcement. Worldly achievement hinges on passionate ardor. They who keep the world from stagnation, who strike out new paths, inaugurate new eras of progress, who inspire others to action, and overriding apparent impossibilities, accomplish success and leave a monument to their glory through the ages, are characterized by intense enthusiasm.

"Others had as clear convictions of the world's sufferings as Howard. It was passionate ardor that begat his active philanthropy. Erasmus saw the corruptions of Rome as clearly as Luther. Melanchthon apprehended the truths of the gospel from which the church had so widely departed as clearly as Luther; but there were needed Luther's great impulsive nature and fiery energy to stir Europe, and bring on the beginning of the end. Many pious souls saw and deplored the depressed state of religion in the early part of the last century in Great Britain, but it was the flaming zeal and holy ardor of the Wesleys and Whitefield that kindled a kindred enthusiasm among the masses, and breathed life into the dead.

"This zeal, to the fullest, sublimest degree, possessed John Ellison Vassar—familiarly styled, 'Uncle John'—zeal for his Master, zeal for souls, steady, continuous, persistent, tireless, from conversion to glory.

"The universal church of today, from the highest to the most humble member, may study with profit the character of this humble man of God.

"In the winter of 1877 the writer, exhausted with the labor incident to a widely-extended work of grace in Coxsackie-on-the-Hudson, looked abroad for help. The Episcopalian Tyng sent the Baptist Vassar to assist in this Methodist revival. Uncle John belonged to the universal church. He was now near the close of his career. In energy, zeal, and success, we have never seen his equal. He was preeminent in personal contact with men, house-to-house visitation, and in the social meeting. The remembrance is a benediction and an inspiration.

"This land needs today a hundred thousand John Vassars. The same mighty faith, loyalty, and love to Jesus, thorough consecration, unbroken prayer, fulness, Bible intimacy, tender sympathy, and quenchless ardor, would fashion and inspire them for kindred service. *The world is hungry.*

"May the reader be clothed with the mantle that fell from the ascending, triumphant hero, Dec. 6, 1878!"

From the *Christian Age*, London, Eng.

"There is a great deal in a name. General Taylor will always be remembered as old 'Rough and Ready.' The fiery Puritan of the Southern army, Jackson, was well described as 'Stone-wall.' Uncle John Vassar, the celebrated colporteur of the American Tract Society, who tramped America over from one ocean to the other, was known as the 'Shepherd's Dog.'

"He did not claim to be a shepherd, for he put great power upon an educated and ordained ministry. He regarded himself only as a faithful dog, hunting after the stray sheep of the Master's flock, and endeavoring to bring into the fold those Christless souls who were wandering over the devil's commons.

"I have known some extraordinary Christian workers in my day, but I count Uncle John Vassar, Dr. Andrew Bonar of Scotland, and D. L. Moody, to be the three men preeminently who could always season their conversation with gospel salt, and yet never incur the suspicion of cant. They all overflowed with the love of Jesus, and out of the abundance of the heart the mouth spoke the right word at the right moment.

"America is filled with racy anecdotes about Uncle John—as the missionary of Dutchess County, as the colporteur over the prairies of Illinois, as the loving laborer in the Union camps, and as the instructor of negro freedmen clear down to Florida. He was really one of the most remarkable men the American church has yet produced. I never talked with him ten minutes without feeling the electric spark of his piety.

"As I contemplate this life, and see what one 'Shepherd's dog' could do in looking after the stray sheep I am more than ever impressed with the prodigious power of *godly laymen*. Say what we will, there are not a tenth part as many ordained ministers as the immense field demands. There are a hundred things which we ministers cannot do; and unless the million or more servants of Christ outside of the pulpit do these needful things, then this generation of souls will be the awful losers. John Vassar supplied the 'missing link' between the pulpit and the people. His was genuine soul-hunting and soul-winning work. He absolutely did more positive service for the Master than some evangelists who peregrinate the land addressing crowded auditories. He dealt with individuals, and that is the key-note of permanent success.

"Why do not thousands of other laymen and women enact the blessed part of 'shepherds' dogs,' like Uncle John? Even if they do not turn colporteurs, why can they not lay hold of the unconverted around them, and, with fervent prayer, 'pull them out of the fire'? We fear that the sad, honest reason is that they do not love their Lord, and do not yearn for the salvation of souls, as that grand old man did who was laid last winter in his grave beside the Hudson. His last word was 'Hallelujah!' It was the first note in his song of glory for having turned many to righteousness. The old 'shepherd's dog' will find his rescued sheep before Immanuel's throne."

From the *Pittsburgh Advocate.*

"The piety of John Vassar was real, radiant, and beautiful. It gleamed with celestial light. It shone with the glory of God. At the foot of the cross Uncle John found strength, sympathy, inspiration, and all the elements of success. He could not be discouraged or repressed, for he realized constantly the presence and power of the Highest. He gave his life to the business of placing living stones in that ever-growing temple which enshrines the glory of the divine presence, and which is destined to fill the whole earth and to lift its gorgeous dome to the summit of the heavens.

"The world needs Christianity; it needs a real Christianity; it needs a personal Christianity. It is not enough to be able to point to a dogma or an experience, and say, *'That* is Christianity.' The evidence must be personal and living. The testimony, *'He* shows forth the genuine gospel,' is the testimony which cannot be gainsaid or resisted. It is the embodied gospel which smites and saves. Infidelity cannot stand before it. Holiness in the heart, in the life, on the lip, in flowing tears, in melting tones, in self-denying labors, in generous outpouring for others, is the greatest power known among men.

"The impossible argument to answer is the argument of a holy life. He who lives in God and for God transmits that life, of necessity, to his fellow-men. The life of John Vassar was a life of constant prayer. The apostle's ideal of devoutness, 'Pray without ceasing,' was with him, perhaps, as nearly a realization as with any man who has ever lived. He prayed day and night, before he went out and when he came in, in private and in public, in spirit and in word. He turned his life into prayer. He interceded for the chureh, and he groaned before God in behalf of the unsaved. 'Praying in the Holy Ghost' was an exercise which he seemed to understand.

"Such a communion with God is power with men. Such fervent, clinging friendship for the Messiah produces the deepest tenderness and love for the souls whom the Messiah has redeemed. Men saw that he was not of this world. There was not a particle of gloom or moroseness in his Christian life. That is not a genuine experience of God which repels even. The godliness of some persons is awful, and even hideous. They make religion seem a dreadful thing. When Jesus came down from the mount, his face glinted with the glory of the Father; the people 'were greatly amazed,' but they 'came running to him.' They were attracted, not repelled.

"Some one said that Jesus never smiled, and a little girl answered, 'But he said, "Suffer little children to come unto me," and if he hadn't smiled, they wouldn't have come.' The logic is irresistible. Jesus filled his soul with real experiences which constantly overflowed for the cheer and the salvation of others. The truth is never so mighty as when flashed from devout souls. It is thus that the Lord writes his epistles in letters of light."

From the *Illustrated Christian Weekly.*

"We went, December 9th, seventy miles, through a driving snowstorm, to join with others in laying away in the grave the wornout body of a plain, unlettered, and humble man. Others were there before us, and from greater distances, and hundreds upon hundreds of the most distinguished citizens of our own city, with 'many ministers of different denominations, were waiting to do honor to the memory of this simple layman. Every mouth was giving utterance to his worth, every tongue telling of his amazing work. Every heart was full of thanksgiving for his life, and tears that he was gone. A solemnity was upon each face, a hush upon the city, for John E. Vassar was dead.

"And as this word goes out over the land, there will be sad hearts and weeping eyes in Maine and California, in Minnesota and Florida, and in every state between, and this, too, in thousands of households. Whence this widespread and profound interest in the death of a humble layman who had neither birth nor wealth nor culture to command the attention of his age or nation? What were the elements of power in the life of Mr. Vassar which made him, as we think, the most laborious and the most useful Christian layman of his age ?

"He was a *sincere* man.

"He appeared to be thoroughly honest in his aims, and he was what he appeared to be. Free from guile, pure of heart, and undisguisedly frank and straightforward in his purpose, he impressed all as a true-hearted man.

"On this cornerstone of unfeigned sincerity was his character builded, and from it sprang many of his noblest traits. It made him frank in commendation, fearless in reproof, unflinching in maintaining the right, and gently firm in reclaiming the erring.

"He was an *earnest* man.

"With an object before him, his entire being was aflame that he might accomplish it. No obstacle was too great to be hurled out of the way, no difficulty too high to be surmounted when with intense zeal he undertook work for Christ; and for thirty years he had no other work to do. His soul was on fire to save souls and with an intensity of desire which consumed him he worked to that end. This made him magnetic in action, fervent in prayer, convincing in argument, resistless in appeal.

"With the little children he became as a little child, and softly led them to their Elder Brother. To the inquiring, but timid boy, to the shrinking and trembling girl, he talked so frankly and lovingly, that they soon gained confidence and told him of their difficulties in finding Christ. The gay and thoughtless young man could not escape the directness of his appeals nor the point of his exhortation. The scoffing infidel cowered before his gentle, but indignant rebuke, and the hardened skeptic, physician or lawyer, was often foiled by his shrewd retort or his burning logic.

"His labor was diligent, but his appeals for the Holy Spirit were unceasing. As he walked the street, as he entered the house, as he sat down, as he rose up, when he fell asleep, when he awoke in the night, as he dressed in the morning, always and everywhere his petition was going up, 'Blessed Jesus, save souls, save these souls.' Here and in the constant study of Holy Scripture was the hiding of his power. Thus he was wise to win souls.

"He was a *large-hearted* man.

22

"Few men escape entirely from the restricting circumstances of early education and the narrowing effect of prejudice; very few conquer the bias and prepossessions of peculiar training.

"This combination of characteristics—sincerity, earnestness, and large-heartedness, all consecrated to the one Master, Christ—all devoted to the one end, the glory of Christ—all suffused, energized, and directed by the Spirit of Christ—made 'Uncle John' Vassar the most godly, the most laborious, and the most successful lay missionary we have ever known. The church of God is poorer, and heaven is enriched by his translation."

It is eminently fitting that a resident of Poughkeepsie should tell of the estimate put upon the man and his work at home; so let the senior pastor of the city, Dr. F. B. Wheeler, put the following testimonial on the closing pages of this book.

"Poughkeepsie is honored in having been the birthplace and residence of John E. Vassar—the place where he was born into the kingdom of God's grace, and whence he went into the kingdom of God's glory.

"This city caught the first fervor of his new life, and witnessed the earnest, heroic sacrifices of his first consecration. Here he began to pray. Here he put on the armor of a true Christian knighthood. Here began those labors which widened with the years into the most substantial and blessed results. From this city the sower went forth to sow beside all waters, and from it the sower and reaper ascended laden with sheaves.

"We feel that we have been like the two disciples to whom the Lord joined Himself in their morning walk. 'Their eyes were holden that they should not know Him.' So we, though we saw the shining of his face, and were stirred by his words, and were borne on the breath of his prayers, and were made familiar with his simple and unworldly life, scarcely knew the man till he vanished from our sight. We find ourselves dwelling upon his character with feelings akin to reverence, and marvel at that grace of God which made possible and real such a life—a life so closely patterned after our blessed Lord that, as we think of it, it rises before us as an incarnation of saintly tenderness. The writer of these lines knew him intimately for the last twenty years of his life, and knew him as a man of clean integrity, catholic in spirit, an enthusiasm that many waters could not quench, and a piety of wonderful fervor and fragrance.

"Love for the Lord Christ and for souls was the master, consuming passion of his life. During these years of our acquaintance he was occupied in fields remote, but from his exhausting labors he would frequently return to gather up and rebind the activities which had been so severely taxed, in the quiet of his Poughkeepsie home. But the man of God, instead of resting, would throw himself into our religious movements with such a flame of devotion as to make his presence like the Shekinah of God's glory. Again and again at such times my knowledge of his return would first be had by his presence in my study, with the earnest inquiry, 'How is it with dear old Poughkeepsie?' And then, after a few words of his growing experience and enlarging views, 'Let us have a season of prayer,' falling upon his knees, pouring out such utterances as lifted one into the very presence of God. From these interviews he would go forth into the streets and homes of the city, beseeching men to be reconciled to God. With us, as elsewhere, he was the man of one idea, to which all things were subordinated. The Lord Christ was ever in his thoughts, and His praise upon his lips. For reasons that are obvious, he labored more abundantly, and with larger success, abroad than in Poughkeepsie. Measurably of him it was true as of others, 'A prophet is not without honor save in his own country;' but for all that, there was no man in Poughkeepsie more respected and beloved than John E. Vassar. He lived and died among us as a man of unquestioned piety, to whom all gave honor.

"It was not hard for him to get at men—he found his way straight to their hearts. His words awakened no opposition, and roused no argument, such was the tenderness of his appeals and the manly consistency of his life. I think the general conviction here, for years, ever since his conversion, has been that, however it might be with other men, piety with John E. Vassar was a living fact. And yet there was nothing morose and forbidding about the man. Loving and gentle in all his ways, he drew you to himself in the sweetest and most perfect of confidences. Better than this, he so put the loving Lord before you that you felt you could almost see the face that once was marred, and grasp the dear hand that was pierced for your sins.

"His religion had none of the weakness of mere sentiment, rhapsody, or cant about it, but came upon you like a strong, fresh breath from the everlasting hills of God. In it strength and beauty were so mingled as to constitute a sturdy and attractive character.

"But it was the simplicity of the man, and his self-renouncing, that commended him to all and made him a wonderful force. Whatever came from his efforts, he was accustomed to speak of it as God-produced, through the feeblest instrumentality—all of God and through God—he nothing but a poor sinner saved by grace. Whatever formulated religious belief he had was pre-eminently Biblical in matter and form, for with him the Word of God was ultimate and supreme authority. The type of his religion was apostolic from core to surface. As to the Lord Jesus, he crowned Him Lord of lords and King of kings, giving to Him without stint the homage of an undivided and loyal heart.

"He was not a great man in the ordinary reckoning of greatness. His education was limited, his personal presence not commanding, and in intellectual grasp and genius he was inferior to many men; but in

22*

those spiritual characteristics which make a man a prince with God, few were his equals.

"Among the pleasant memories of my life is my acquaintance with this saint. Among the sweet and lifting hopes that reach beyond the shadows is that of greeting him again. Poughkeepsie will cherish the memory of that Vassar whose munificence founded a college, and it will not forget that other Vassar who lived and walked with God—the man who has turned many to righteousness, who has given to the world a most signal illustration of the power of a Christian faith. He was twice born in Poughkeepsie; he lived here, here he died, and here his mortal dust sleeps. Herein is honor for which we thank God, counting this honor inferior to none other which God has given us. 'The Lord shall count, when He writeth up the people, that *this man* was born there.'

> Gone at last, to be with Jesus,
>   Lord of life, and Prince of peace;
> Through his loving-kindness precious,
>   Found from sorrow glad release.
> Darkness all now disappearing,
>   Comes the bright eternal day,
> With its light forever shining
>   Cloud and night have passed away.
>
> Lo, the King in all his glory
>   Greets the servant in the skies;
> Visions of surpassing beauty
>   Flash upon him in surprise.
> Oh! the beatific meeting
>   Of the glorified above,
> One, who long in labor serving,
>   Wrought with zeal and burning love.

Brother, hail! forever ransomed
  From the thrall of earthly care;
Cross and burden now abandoned,
  Robes majestic thou dost wear;
Royal harvests yet shall greet thee
  From the fields that thou hast wwrought
Souls arrested, brought to glory,
  By the lessons thou hast taught.

F. B. W.

POUGHKEEPSIE, N. Y., 1879.

And now this life thus outlined we leave to speak. To speak *for* Christ, to speak *to* men. Many hands have helped to sketch it. Possibly some features may appear to have been overdrawn. To eulogize, however, or in the least degree exaggerate, has been neither the desire nor the design. To present the man just as he was has been the steady aim. And that not that he might be magnified, but "to the praise of the glory of His grace."

It has been the hope and prayer that through the man his Master might be seen—that Master who made him what he was.

The beauty of holiness, and the blessedness of service, and the grandeur of sacrifice, are the lessons of his life.

This is the call which it sounds in the ears of every soldier of the Lord: Sink self out of sight in Christ. Warn, persuade, entreat men to be reconciled to God. Pray, wrestle, believe, and through the might of the indwelling Spirit turn others from sin to righteousness, and thus thin perdition and people Paradise.

So shall the heart keep full of holy joy. So shall life look bright from a dying bed. So shall the wandering and the lost be found. So shall the Father be glorified. So shall the Son see of the travail of His soul.

> "Let us draw their mantles o'er us
>   Which have fallen in our way.
> Let us do the work before us
>   Calmly, bravely, while we may;
> Ere the long night-silence cometh
>   And with us it is not day."

UNCLE JOHN VASSAR,
OR
THE FIGHT OF FAITH.
12 mo., Cloth, $1.00.

"We believe that the volume is destined to carry on the good work which its subject begun." —*The Congregationalist.*

"If one wants to know how to be wholly the Lord's, how to live for Him, to talk about Him, to think of Him, to commune with Him all the time, yet without any appearance of cant, or any lack of naturalness and hearty enjoyment of life, let him by all means read ' Uncle John Vassar, or The Fight of Faith.' " —*Sunday School Times.*

"In my opinion it is one of the most inspiring and soul quickening biographies which this country has produced in many a year. It will be an inspiration to many a pastor and to many a prayer meeting. There ought to be 50,000 copies of this glorious book circulated.' "
Rev. T. L. Cuyler, D. D.

"It is a most delightful, suggestive biography." *-The Contributor.*

"No one can read these pages, crowded with incident, and not receive a new inspiration in Christian work. —*Zion's Advocate.*

"It is difficult to lay down this tender biography until one reaches the last page. It is full of the love of Christ and the love of souls." —*Alabama Baptist.*

"We know of no life-record that is so well calculated to stir the hearts of Christians, and rouse them to whole-souled activity as this." —*The Watchword.*

"The memoir of ' Uncle John' is the most thrilling bit of Christian biography of the time. It is an inspiration for any one to read it. For myself, I turned from its pages thanking God for such a nineteenth century apostle, and with a great new desire to serve his Master and mine." *Rev. Geo. F. Pentecost.*

"The best of all ways to raise up such men as Uncle John, is by the wide-spread circulation of this admirable memoir, the reading of which can scarcely fail to quicken the most sluggish Christian pulse to a quicker, healthier beat." —*The Baptist Teacher.*

"Few books which have crossed the Atlantic will command a larger number of grateful and admiring readers than that which sets forth the life of ' Uncle John Vassar.' "
—*From Rev. Charles H. Spurgeon's "Sword and Trowel."*

"John Vassar is portrayed vividly. One can almost see him. Yet he is nowhere a hero in himself. Between the lines one sees the Master he served. A painter may exhaust his art upon the glory of the clouds at sunset, yet every stroke of his brush reveals the glory of the sun, and honors *it* more than it does the cloud. So the writer, as 'Uncle John' would have wished, has given the glory to the Master." —*Journal and Messenger.*

"Like the saintly man himself, it will carry a benediction wherever it goes."
—*Zion's Herald.*

"Christian worker, read this volume if you would have kindled in your bosom a fresh inspiration for more zealous *personal* work for the Master."
—*Y. M. C. A. Watchman.*

"It is a wonderful life, and the story as here told is one of the most powerful arguments for the Christian religion which men can read. The book ought to find its way into every household in the land." —*The Morning Star.*

"My soul has been blessed by it. The world will be better for such a book. I thank God for this new influence to the unsaved, and the spiritual elevation of our race."
—*G. J.Johnson, D. D.*

"It is indeed a valuable ' means of grace' to read such a record."
—*The London Christian.*

"We have very rarely read more valuable matter than this book contains. No one can read it without profit." —*Christian Worker.*

"Through this excellent book John Vassar's Christian soul will work on."
—*Christian Advocate.*

"It is refreshing to read such a book, and it helps one to believe still in the regenerating power of the old-fashioned gospel, and the devotion of spirit which characterizes the true apostle and preacher of Christ everywhere." —*Church and People.*

"I have read it with delight, and, I hope, spiritual profit. It moved me to tears of self-condemnation and aspiration after a better life." *Henry G. Weston, D. D. President of Crozer Theo. Sem.*

"All who read this life will be impressed with the beauty of holiness, the blessedness of service, and the grandeur of sacrifice as herein displayed."
—*Western Christian Advocate.*

"The story of his life is like a beam of light streaming through darkness."
—*The Standard.*

"The narrative of his conversion and work must prove a blessing to hundreds."
—*Lutheran Observer.*

"We have noticed no production of this character of late years which utters such vigorous and practical Christianity in industrial life. " —*Christian World.*

"Emphatically this book cannot be read too much or lived enough."
—*Syracuse Advocate.*

"Every student in every Theological Seminary in the land should have a copy. Every pastor in the land would be quickened by its perusal." —*Christian Secretary.*

"A wonderful life—a life worthliving. It will be translated in other languages, that the church and world may know what one good man may do for Christ." —*The Observer.*

"His life ought to be read by tens of thousands of Christians. It is full of encitement, of instruction and encouragement. It is a pleasure to notice a book that can be so heartily and unreservedly commended." —*Christian Intelligencer.*

"It is a most quickening biography." —*The Presbyterian.*

"The whole book is an incentive to the service of Christ in any condition and sphere of life in which the Christian may be placed." —*The Episcopal Recorder.*

"No Christian man or woman can afford *not* to read it." —*Illus. Christian Weekly.*

"The life of 'Uncle John Vassar' is here drawn in glowing colors, with a tender, true hand. He speaks again from its pages, and the words breathe his spirit and his zeal. We hope every young man in the nation will read this work and learn its lesson of real greatness, which is, doing noble things, not dreaming them." —*Church Union.*

"It is one of the most interesting and inspiring books we have ever read. We sincerely wish that every Christian could be persuaded to read it" —*Vermont Baptist.*

"Such a book cannot fail to be read by many thousands, and it is pleasant to think no one can read it without a new impulse in the life that leads ever upward ." —*The Watch Tower.*

"It is a beautiful picture of a noble Christian life." —*The Interior.*

"It will be wise for pastors to give it a wide circulation among their people, to promote personal piety and to kindle zeal for labor." —*The Watchman.*

"This simple story of his life and work deserves wide circulation."
—*Evangelical Magazine, London.*

"It is certainly refreshing reading in these times, when scepticism is doing so much to undermine Christianity. A life like that of Uncle John Vassar does much to silence the voice of infidelity." —*Christian Herald.*

"Let Christians who want stimulus in their religious career read it. Let parents who want their children to pattern after a good model, place this book in their hands."
—*Evangelical Messenger.*

"It is one of the most charming biographies that we have ever read. It is an eloquent argument from his consecrated life for a deeper experience in religion, for greater fellowship with Christ and for greater Christian activity."
—*Baptist Weekly.*

*** May be ordered of any Bookseller in the U. S. or England.